THE PUZZLE OF THE GOSPELS

The Puzzle of the Gospels

PETER VARDY AND MARY MILLS

Fount
An Imprint of HarperCollinsPublishers

Fount Paperbacks is an Imprint of
HarperCollins*Religious*
Part of HarperCollins*Publishers*
77–85 Fulham Palace Road, London W6 8JB

First published in Great Britain
in 1995 by Fount Paperbacks

1   3   5   7   9   10   8   6   4   2

A catalogue record for this book
is available from the British Library

ISBN 0 00 627878-7

Printed and bound in Great Britain by
HarperCollinsManufacturing Glasgow

TO ANNE MURPHY SHCJ AND PEGGY MOORE

CONTENTS

PART FIVE – THE QUESTION OF TRUTH

ACKNOWLEDGEMENTS

Responsibility for all errors lies entirely with the authors but there would have been more of them were it not for the proof-reading efforts and advice of the following to whom the authors are very grateful: Fr Robert Murray SJ; Martin Poulson SDB; Paul O'Reilly SJ, Peggy Moore, Anne and Catherine Vardy and Anne Laing-Brooks. Biblical quotations are from the New Revised Standard Version except where indicated otherwise.

MARY MILLS SHCJ
PETER VARDY

Easter 1994 to Epiphany 1995

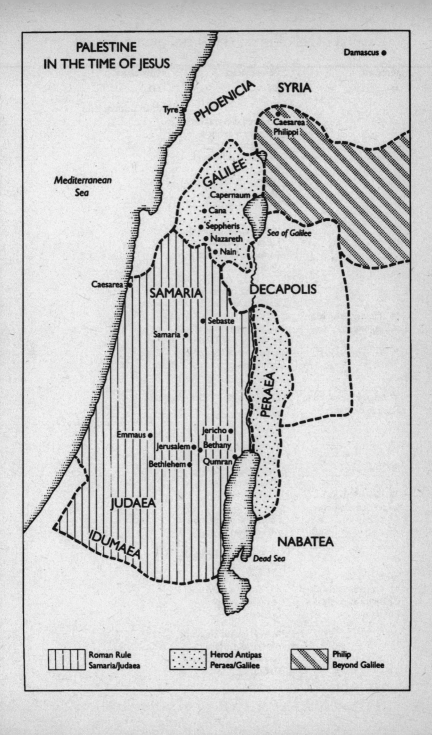

PALESTINE
IN THE TIME OF JESUS

Damascus ●

PHOENICIA   SYRIA

Tyre ●

Caesarea
Philippi ●

Mediterranean
Sea

GALILEE

Capernaum ●
● Cana
● Seppheris   Sea of Galilee
● Nazareth
● Nain

Caesarea ●

SAMARIA   DECAPOLIS

● Sebaste

Samaria ●

PERAEA

Emmaus ●   Jericho ●

Jerusalem ●   ● Bethany
Bethlehem ●   ● Qumran

JUDAEA

IDUMAEA   NABATEA

Dead Sea

| ‖‖‖ Roman Rule Samaria/Judaea | ⋯ Herod Antipas Peraea/Galilee | ⧄ Philip Beyond Galilee |

MAJOR DATES OF INTEREST IN THE FIRST CENTURY

Roman	Palestinian	Christian
AD	AD	AD
		6/4? Birth of Jesus
	4 Herod dies and his territory is divided among his sons: Antipas, (Galilee and Peraea) Philip (Northern Transjordan) Archelaus (Judea, Idumea, Samaria)	
	6 Archelaus removed and Judea annexed by Romans. Census of Quirinius	
	10 Inauguration of Caesarea by Herod	
14 Tiberius succeeds as Emperor	c.20 Herod Antipas founds city of Tiberias in honour of the Emperor	
27 Augustus establishes Roman Empire	26–36 Pontius Pilate procurator of Judea	
		30/33 Crucifixion of Jesus
	34 Death of Philip, the tetrarch of Transjordan Philo Jewish theologian c15BC–45CE/AD	
37 Gaius Caligula succeeds as Emperor		
	38 Jewish pogroms in Alexandria	
	40 Removal of Herod Antipas	
41 Caligula assassinated Claudius succeeds as Emperor	41 Threat to desecrate Jerusalem temple averted	
	41–44 Jewish kingdom of Herod Agrippa I (grandson of Herod the Great)	

MAJOR DATES OF INTEREST IN THE FIRST CENTURY

Roman	Palestinian	Christian
AD	AD	AD
	44 Death of Agrippa I. Roman rule of Jewish province by procurators reintroduced	
		49 Council in Jerusalem
		51 Paul appears before Gallio in Corinth
	52–62 Felix governor in Palestine. Succeeded by Porcius Festus	
54 Nero succeeds as Emperor		
		64 Persecutions of Roman Christians
	66 Outbreak of Jewish War against Rome	
68 Year of the 4 Emperors		
69 Vespasian succeeds as Emperor	70 Destruction of Jerusalem by Titus. Temple tax diverted to Rome	
	73 Fall of Masada (suicide of defenders)	
	75/79 Josephus' account of *Jewish War* published	
79 Titus succeeds as Emperor		
81 Domitian succeeds as Emperor		Main period of Christian persecution under Domitian. John's exile to Patmos (Book of Revelation)
	85 Rabbinic council at Jamnia	

PART 1

INTRODUCTION

ONE

Two Stories

The gospels tell a story. There are many types of story ranging from fiction through biographies to attempts at historical accounts. Even so-called 'true' stories will be affected by the perception of the writer.

In the 1980s, a man advertised for a woman to spend a year with him on a desert island. Their year together resulted in two books – one written by the man and one by the woman. Although both said that they were giving an account of what happened in the year, the pictures that emerged were radically different because in the two cases the stories were being presented from a particular viewpoint. It is impossible to present any book without taking the viewpoint of the author into account – which is one reason why this book will be devoting considerable time to understanding the purpose and intention of the individual gospel writers. Matthew, Mark, Luke and John present different accounts of the life and death of Jesus of Nazareth, as one might expect from four people who, although they use some common material, nevertheless present this material in distinctive ways.

Some may reject this kind of careful examination of the gospels saying that there is no 'puzzle' – they are the word of God. However it is not as simple as that. The gospels were written by human beings. There is no suggestion in Christianity, as there is in Islam, that the gospels were divinely dictated. Jesus' friends and the followers of his friends wrote down accounts of his life and these accounts differ. The gospels present a particular problem for twentieth-century readers as there are no similar texts in ancient literature – they are not straightforward biographies.

This book will be concerned with helping you, the reader, to understand the gospel stories and how they came to be written; to bring to light the implicit references that were being made of which modern readers may be unaware; and also to consider the issue of the truth of the stories. 'Truth' can sometimes be regarded as a dirty word by some biblical scholars who see themselves primarily as experts on the literary documents with which they are dealing. However this is to ignore the basic questions about the sort of story the gospels are meant to represent. One cannot ignore the issue of whether the gospel writers were intending to make claims to truth and, if so, what sort of claims these were. Part of the puzzle of the gospels is to work out what story is being presented to the reader, but there is then an equally important question: to what extent and in what way should the stories be regarded as true rather than fictional accounts?

One story

Imagine you live a thousand years in the future and you are doing historical research on London between 1850 and 1900. One character whose name you come across is Sherlock Holmes. Various books had been written about him, many of them by a man called Arthur Conan Doyle, and records of these books are still retained. A few copies of early editions of these books are still in existence, carefully preserved in temperature-controlled conditions. In some of these books there are references to other stories which are no longer available.

It is clear that this man lived in an area of London called Baker Street. Archaeological research in parts of London (underneath the destruction caused by several wars in the thousand intervening years) revealed a station which was used by trains which ran on rails underground. There were mosaics on the walls of this station showing a man in a hat smoking a pipe and these matched the description given of Sherlock Holmes and pictures of him in some of the preserved books. Other pictures gave a different appearance. This station was re-built in 1985, in other words about sixty to ninety years after the stories of Sherlock Holmes were written. This seemed to the archaeologists to point to the truth of the stories as the man must have been revered many years after he died. What is more, old telephone books showed records of a Sherlock Holmes Society indicating that the man must have had followers. Further excavations in the area uncovered a house and a broken, blue plaque which seemed to commemorate Sherlock Holmes. There were even television programmes made about him, the details of which corresponded to the stories in the books.

The archaeologists carefully checked the details in the stories against the records available about life in Britain under Queen Victoria. The details seemed accurate – there were taxi-cabs called Hansoms pulled by horses; there were many young boys who did not go to school; the medical details given in the books corresponded to the records available of medical research at the time. Holmes was recorded in the books as smoking a drug and this drug was available in London at the time. He travelled on railways and both the places he travelled to and the railways existed. Moreover, Holmes apparently smoked a pipe and the practice of smoking nicotine, even though because of its harmful effects it had disappeared hundreds of years in the past, seemed to have been common in London at the time Holmes was meant to have lived. All the details seemed to be accurate.

The question arose as to whether the stories about Sherlock Holmes were true. There were different views on the question. Some experts at one extreme held that the stories were certainly true and cited the number of facts that could be verified. Experts at the other extreme said that the stories were entirely works of fiction, although they admitted that many of the details in the stories seemed to be true. A third group thought that whilst the details of the stories might have been elaborated over the years, nevertheless the main thrust of the stories was true: there must, indeed, have been a detective called Sherlock Holmes and he must have had a friend called Dr Watson who recorded the details of his cases. Not all the details were necessarily correct, but doctors were careful men and it seemed likely that most of the details were accurate. A fourth group rejected the existence of a man called Sherlock Holmes but nevertheless said that the stories were true in that they showed how detective work should be carried out. The 'genius' of Sherlock Holmes (shown in his methods of examination of evidence, careful deduction and attention to detail) was as valid in the year 3000 as in the year 2000 – or in 1900.

Yet another group had a radical theory. They maintained that Sherlock Holmes never existed, but he was modelled on a friend of Arthur Conan Doyle who had the same powers of deduction as the fictional Sherlock Holmes. They suggested that Conan Doyle studied medicine and they even found old hospital records which indicated that as a student doctor he had indeed studied medicine under someone called Dr Joseph Bell. They therefore suggested that Dr Bell might have been the model for Holmes.

Disputes between the various groups and their offshoots were fierce. Many learned articles were written and professors were appointed to universities based on their skill in writing new books and developing new theories on the subject. There seemed no clear answers and the more people read, the more confused they became about the issue. None of the people who studied the records became detectives – their lives were devoted to literary and archaeological analysis.

Another story

In many ways, the story about Jesus is similar to that about Sherlock Holmes. Many of the details given of life at the time of Jesus seem to be accurate. Disputes about the story are considerable and there is a very wide range of views about the status of this story and its truth. Many learned articles and books have been written on the subject by professors, Doctors of Theology and many different types of priest, but we are no nearer a consensus view. Every ten years a new theory emerges which, briefly, attracts headline attention before being replaced by yet another 'new' idea.

How, if at all, does the Jesus story in the gospels differ from the Sherlock Holmes story? There is little evidence outside the gospels on which to draw for details about Jesus. The three most important sources are the following. Pliny wrote to the Roman emperor, Trajan, in 111 AD about Christians he met in north-east Asia Minor and said:

> They meet on a certain fixed day before sunrise and sing an antiphonal hymn to Christ as God, and bind themselves with an oath – not to commit any crime, but to abstain from all acts of theft, robbery and adultery, and from breaches of trust . . . . (Pliny, Letter 10, 96)

Trajan, a Roman historian, wrote in about 116 AD about the Christians who were blamed by Nero for the fire which swept through Rome in 64 AD. He says:

> They got their name from Christ, who was executed by sentence of the procurator Pontius Pilate in the reign of Tiberius. (*Annals* 15, 44, 2)

The earliest comment was by the Jewish historian, Josephus, who took part in the Jewish resistance to Rome in 64 AD. However, although he probably wrote about 85–95 AD the surviving manuscript of his writings is dated much later and Christian writers had almost certainly altered the text. Josephus refers to John the Baptist and to the stoning to death of 'the brother of Jesus, the so-called Christ – James by name' in 62 AD. Graham Stanton suggests that the original comments of Josephus about Jesus may have been on the following lines:

> About this time lived Jesus, a wise man, a teacher of those who delight in accepting the truth (or the unusual). He attracted many

Jews, and also many from the Greek world. He was the so-called Christ. On the accusation of our leading men, Pilate condemned him to the cross, but those who were attracted to him from the first did not cease to love him. The race of Christians named after him has survived to this day. (*The Gospels and Jesus*, p. 143)

None of these sources adds to the story about Jesus given in the gospels and, effectively, the gospels are the only real source of information about Jesus' life, although some brief confirmation may be obtained from Paul's letters written between fifteen and thirty years after Jesus' death. Essentially, however, the gospel stories themselves are the only real source.

It is all very well asking 'Are the gospels true?', but although this question seems simple it becomes much more complex when it is examined. Firstly it is not clear what is meant by 'the gospel story'. As we will see, there are four different accounts and in some cases these accounts differ. The gospel writers disagree on many of the details and this is to be expected given that they were human beings writing some time after the events they describe. In a way the differences support rather than undermine the accounts as the differences are what might be expected from human writers relying on the oral and written sources available to them and writing at a distance of a few years from the events.

It is not possible to arrive at a single 'Life of Jesus' given the differences between the gospel writers and the complexities of the different narratives, but this does not mean that there is not a coherent story that emerges from the four texts. The more one descends into the detail, the more argument there may be and this shows the danger of relying too greatly on specific words attributed to Jesus. Specific sayings attributed to Jesus, or even accounts of events in his life, may be:

a) true exactly as described,
b) broadly true, although the evangelist may have altered the emphasis to make particular theological points, or

c) not true in any literal sense, but instead conveying the early
  churches' impression of what Jesus might have said in particular
  situations or what they thought about Jesus.

By itself a) is not a viable option, at least not for every single verse of
all four gospels. Either Jesus' ministry lasted one year or three years;
either John's chronology of the events leading up to Jesus' death and
crucifixion is correct or the account given in the Synoptics is true
(cf. pp. 72–5). However a) and b) are compatible. Some accounts
may be true exactly as described whilst others may have been the
result of a theological gloss by the evangelist. Those who take
option c) would see Jesus as similar to Sherlock Holmes or perhaps
Hamlet or Macbeth. They might claim that there was an actual man
called Jesus, but may hold that the stories that have been embroi-
dered around him have little or no contact with his actual life. The
real choice is between a) and b) on the one hand and c) on the other,
and the two alternatives may both apply in different areas.

   Experts today differ just as much about the truth of the Jesus story
as the 'experts' a thousand years hence may disagree about Sherlock
Holmes. Therefore this book has two main objectives:

1   To try to explain what can be deduced from the four stories
about Jesus which are available today in the gospels of Matthew,
Mark, Luke and John – after taking into account the latest biblical
scholarship and the balance of evidence. There is no question that
these four stories are great pieces of literature and that they have a
story to tell. However it is not always clear precisely what story this
is and unless one understands the background against which the
gospel writers wrote their texts, it is not possible to understand their
different stories. This book will aim to help in the task of understanding the gospel stories and will try to explore the limits of what
can and cannot be said about them.

2   To ask how the issue of 'the truth of the gospel stories' might be
tackled and whether any conclusions are possible.

This is an introductory book. A tremendous number of learned works have been written about the matters dealt with herein, yet certainty and agreement seem to be as far away as ever. A person could devote their life to studying the gospels and, indeed, many do so.

The four gospels are not simple pieces of literature. They are at the centre of the faith of hundreds of millions of Christians throughout the world. The supposed message of the gospels has caused many wars, has been responsible for persecution and oppression, and has inspired some of the greatest pieces of art, the most sublime music as well as the lives of many of the finest men and women that the world has ever seen. The stories have tremendous significance and arouse the passions.

Having said this, the aim of this book is to be dispassionate, to try to understand the issues and to assess the factors involved without letting the authors' own preconceptions colour the presentation. You, the reader, must make up your own mind about the gospels; about how they should be understood and what your response to them should be. Hopefully, this book will help in this task.

TWO

The Core Ideas in the Gospels

Although this book aims to explore modern understandings of the gospel material, such a study cannot be carried out without understanding the society and setting for which the gospels were written. The Bible aims to communicate religious truth to the reader. Since it was compiled in the ancient world, it conveys its messages by means of the words and ideas which were familiar in that world. Many of these concepts may initially seem strange to the modern reader because they no longer form part of our worldview.

To take gospel study seriously requires attention to the concepts which express the message about Jesus. All the following terms will be found to occur frequently and their understanding will be assumed when the individual gospel stories are described.

Messiah/Son of God

'Messiah' means the same as 'Christ' and both terms mean 'the Anointed One'. Jewish tradition knows of three different types of anointed figure, that of king, priest and prophet. The royal Messiah can be seen, for example, in Psalm 132:17. Here God describes David's sons:

> I will cause a horn to sprout up for David, I have prepared a lamp for my anointed one.

The title 'Anointed One' is given to King David's children who come to the throne of Israel and is intended to show that Israel's kings have been chosen by God. When David's dynasty died out, the hope remained that a descendant of David would appear in the future to govern God's people. What is envisaged here is a human king of equal stature to the heroic David of past legend.

Priests from the time of Aaron (Moses' collaborator in the Exodus from Egypt) were anointed as part of their ordination. The Qumran community documents imply that the members of this community were looking for a renewal of priestly leadership which may have entailed a priestly messiah—leader coming forward to lead the group. Indeed some have argued that Jesus was just such a leader from the Qumran community.

Prophets were anointed to their role as God's spokesmen, generally not with oil but rather with the Spirit of God so that they could literally act as God's spokesmen. For instance, the call of Isaiah (Isaiah 6) and Jeremiah (Jeremiah 1) imply the placing of God's own words in the prophets' mouths.

Usually the term 'Messiah' refers to the first of these categories, in other words to a kingly figure. Psalms 2 and 110 reflect this theme of a king chosen by God and given a new identity together with power over his enemies. Some Jews expected a warrior Messiah who would drive out their enemies and establish a new kingdom like that of David. The gospel writers see Jesus fulfilling this role, albeit in a way that was totally different to Jewish expectations.

Attached to the term 'Messiah' is usually the title 'Son of God'. This term is also used for Israel's king.

> I will raise up your offspring after you, who shall come forth from your body, and I will establish his kingdom. He shall build a house for my name, and I will establish the throne of his kingdom for ever. I will be a father to him, and he shall be a son to me . . . . I will not take my steadfast love from him, as I took it from Saul . . . . Your house and your kingdom shall be made sure forever before me; your throne shall be established forever. (2 Samuel 7:12–16)

'Son of God' is a title which the evangelists, especially Matthew, liked to use about Jesus (cf. p. 23). This does not mean that it should automatically be read literally. As the quotation above makes clear, Jews regarded the King of Israel as 'Son of God'.

Kingdom of God

J. Jeremias (*New Testament Theology 1*, pp. 30–5) has argued that Jesus' language about the 'kingdom of God' has very few parallels in the Judaism of his time. By the 'criterion of dissimilarity' (p. 120) this is likely to have been a key theme of Jesus' teaching.

The first kingdom of God was when God gave the Promised Land to the people who had been captive in Egypt to rule over. God 'owned' the territory included in Israel and Judah in Palestine and chose to give it to the Israelites who were God's own sons, freed from slavery. This lasted, in biblical terms, until the invasion of these kingdoms by the nations of Assyria and Babylon respectively, and some first-century Jews looked for the restoration of this political kingdom.

However Genesis 1 shows that the God of Israel is the God of the whole universe and so another way of looking at God's kingdom is to see it as including the whole cosmos – heaven and earth. All living creatures, all plants and, indeed, the structures of the universe itself are, in this view, included in God's kingdom. A war goes on between God with his angels and the Devil with his angels. It is not clear from the biblical account where the devils came from, although another Jewish text of the period, the book of 1 Enoch (a Jewish text with the oldest parts dating from the third century B.C.), contains the story of how angels defied God's order by coming down from heaven to marry human wives and so brought a sentence of banishment on themselves as enemies of God. Later writers such as Augustine were to see devils as angels who had wilfully misused their freedom and, due to pride, had rebelled against God.

God's eventual kingdom will, according to the gospels, be established when Satan's challenge to God is overthrown, and it is possible to see Jesus as 'God's general' in this war against the forces of darkness. The nature of this kingdom is dealt with in Jesus' parables and these are discussed in Chapter 14.

Son of man

The term 'Son of man' as a title is drawn from Daniel:

> . . . and behold, with the clouds of heaven there came one like a
> son of man, and he came to the Ancient of Days and was
> presented before him. And to him was given dominion and glory
> and kingdom, that all peoples, nations, and languages should
> serve him; his dominion is an everlasting dominion, which shall
> not pass away . . . . (Daniel 7:13–14)

This heavenly figure corresponds to God's faithful people on earth
and he has his own individual identity among God and his court.
Similarly in 1 Enoch, humans are described in coded language as
beasts of various kinds, whilst angels and heavenly beings are
described as 'sons of men' – i.e. having a human form. Part of 1
Enoch is a book modern scholars call *The Similitudes*. Here again a
Son of man figure appears and here, too, the work of this figure is to
bring about God's kingdom and to execute justice. However it is
probably the Daniel passage that was most influential on the gospel
writers – the clear reference to his being given 'glory and kingdom'
by God means that Jesus' identification with the Son of man figure
helps to confirm his pedigree in fulfilling the OT scriptures.

It should be noted that the quotation above is taken from the
Revised Standard Version and not from the New RSV. The point is
significant as the NRSV translates the phrase 'one like the son of
man' as 'one like a human being' and, while the latter is a more
accurate translation of the original Hebrew, the compilers of the
gospels used a Greek translation which has the former meaning, and
thus identify Jesus as 'Son of Man' (Matthew 24:30; 26:64; Mark
13:26; 14:62; Luke 21:27). Some modern commentators prefer the
implications of the modern translation, rather than understanding
the phrase 'Son of Man' as a title.

Moses

Moses was a key figure in first-century Judaism. He was seen as the major founder of Israel and its religion – he was prophet, law-giver, teacher and ruler. Moses saw God face to face and took from God the tablets of stone on which the Laws of Israel were inscribed. Moses became a figure of even greater importance than David since there were no more kings of David's line ruling the country. Any new hero-figure had, therefore, to be compared with Moses and, as is made clear on pp. 25–27, the gospel writers drew parallels between Jesus and Moses.

Temple/house of God

The Temple in Jerusalem is described in some psalms as Mt Zion. According to Israelite teaching, Mt Zion is the name for God's holy mountain-top home. Hence the belief that God lived in the Temple in Jerusalem in a special way. As Psalm 132 says:

> The Lord has chosen Zion; he has desired it for his habitation. (Psalm 132:13)

This idea is connected by the psalmist with David bringing the Ark of the Lord up to Jerusalem (2 Samuel 6). As the Ark progresses into its new home, God is seen to be really present in the Temple, the House of God, where it comes to rest. The psalmist thought that God lived in the city and that the Temple is the equivalent of God's home on Mt Zion and in heaven.

The Temple was to mirror God's home and in 1 Kings 6 and 7 the story of how Solomon built the Temple is told. It had outer courts and a Holy Sanctuary where God was believed to be present. The inner court was decorated to look like a garden and contained a lampstand which symbolized the planets as God's eyes watching the world. The Holy Sanctuary held God's throne on the Mercy Seat with the Ark of God as footstool. This was surrounded by guardian angels symbolized by carved figures such as can be seen in the British Museum's Asiatic section. The Sanctuary was so holy that no one was allowed to enter it, according to biblical Law, except the high priest on the Day of Atonement when he offered a blood sacrifice which was meant to reconcile the people with God.

The Ark had been brought to Jerusalem by David but, according to the OT, it had a long history, having accompanied the people of Israel on their wanderings in the desert after the Exodus from Egypt, then into the land of Israel and in the various wars which followed. The Ark appears to have been a box containing holy objects. This sacred item symbolizes God's own chariot throne as can be seen from Ezekiel 1 where the prophet sees God's throne even in a foreign land.

There is intended, therefore, to be a complete parallel between heaven and the Sanctuary. This is important as it meant that the rituals carried out by the priests in the Temple could be seen as effective because they were carried out in God's presence. This explains why the Temple was a focus for the whole Jewish religion and a place of pilgrimage for Jews as they travelled to visit God's own house.

The bridge between earth and heaven, between God's earthly and heavenly home, was completed by the liturgy of song, drama and sacrifice which went on each day according to a sacred calendar. It is perhaps hard for us today to imagine just how well-known and powerful were the images connected with Temple worship in the time of Jesus. These images could be reused, outside of Temple life, to explain the real meaning of important figures. One of the most obvious places where this occurs is in the Book of Revelation. Indeed the whole idea of God as king on his throne (and, perhaps, the traditionally masculine image of God) stems from the concept of God as a king on his throne in his Temple.

The Temple was rebuilt by King Herod on a massive scale. Indeed the building was not completed until after his death and the death of Jesus. Jesus is recorded as saying:

Do you see these great buildings? Not one stone will be left here upon another, all will be thrown down. (Mark 13:2)

The new Temple was designed on a plan essentially similar to the old one, but it was much larger. It was destroyed in the Roman–Jewish war of 66–70 AD when the Romans tried to effectively destroy Jewish culture. Archaeological remains clearly point to the devastation caused in this war but although the Temple was flattened, the memory of it and of the central part it played in the Jewish religion remained.

Both Judaism and Christianity found ways to include the old values of Temple religion in a new setting (see pp. 89–90 where reference is made to how the Pharisees adapted to this event). In the second-century text of Judaism, the Mishnah, the nation is still organized as a worshipping body and called to ritual purity in spite of the loss of the central building. For the early Christian Church also, the destruction of the Temple was important. At the Council of Jerusalem in *c.* 49 AD, the Acts of the Apostles records a dispute between Paul who wished to take the Christian message to Gentiles and the main Christian leaders who wished Christians to be essentially Jewish. Although this Council decided in Paul's favour, the destruction of the Temple meant that his approach was the only realistic way forward for the early Church. Jesus became the sole focus and the Temple could be seen as irrelevant. The Letter to the Hebrews adapts the image of priesthood so that Jesus is seen as both high priest and sacrifice – one whose death has opened the way for all believers to reach the heavenly sanctuary where they will live for ever as part of God's congregation. In the gospel of John, Jesus' body replaces the Temple building; God is seen to dwell in a *person* rather than in a *house* (John 4:16–26). It may well be that this insight developed after the destruction of the Jerusalem Temple.

*　　*　　*

In this chapter, core ideas which occur in all the gospels have been briefly described. In today's culture we are familiar with many ideas which only need to be mentioned to conjure up vivid images: words like the holocaust, nuclear fall-out, the greenhouse effect, and inflation are in everyday use. In much the same way, the core ideas outlined in this chapter would have been a fundamental part of the vocabulary of any Jew at the time of Jesus. Unless one understands the significance of these ideas, one will not understand the gospels. It is necessary to enter into the thought-world in which the gospels were written in order to appreciate their significance.

THREE

The Gospel Story of Matthew

Each of the four gospels presents the story of Jesus in its own distinctive way. Much in the four accounts is the same, but there are significant differences in the manner of presentation used by each gospel writer. The same scenes are inserted into the story at different points, and some traditional material is expanded whereas other material is abbreviated. In each case a chronological order is preserved with the climax being the death of Jesus on the cross. Matthew and Luke take the reader from cradle to grave to resurrection. John follows a similar model but does not start with Jesus' birth – instead he starts with Jesus' position as the Word of God which has entered the world. Mark produces the shortest version of the story, beginning with the adult Jesus and ending with the empty tomb. In this and the next three chapters the individual gospel stories will be explained, allowing the concerns of each gospel writer to become apparent.

*   *   *

Matthew's gospel story reflects a particularly Jewish approach to Jesus of Nazareth. This is highlighted by two concerns of Matthew's:

1   To show Jesus as the expected Messiah, understanding this term to indicate a ruler for the Jews who would be descended from the line of King David, a royal dynasty which died out after the fall of Jerusalem to Babylonian forces in the sixth century BC.

2   To show Jesus to be comparable with the great figure of Jewish tradition, Moses. In the OT Moses appears as the saviour of Israel,

21

leading them out of slavery in Egypt and then as a general leading them towards the Promised Land through hostile territory. He also is the person through whom God speaks to Israel, making a covenant with them at Mt Sinai. Jesus is shown by Matthew not only to be the inheritor of Moses' work, but an even greater leader than Moses – one who can give his followers an ultimate interpretation of God's will.

These two themes constantly recur in this gospel. At his birth, Jesus is shown to be descended from David's line; as he begins his last entry into David's city of Jerusalem, Jesus is called upon by a blind beggar as 'Son of David' (20:30). On the other hand, Jesus is said to have come to fulfil the Jewish Law and the writings of the OT prophets (5:17–19). This passage occurs when Jesus is seated on a hillside teaching the crowds about the true meaning of fulfilling the Law in one's everyday life.

Birth

Matthew's birth story first explains the meaning of Jesus by listing the ancestors of Joseph before giving details of Jesus' birth. His purpose in doing this is to establish the relationship of Jesus to Jewish religion by showing him as:

a) a descendant of Abraham whom God promised would be the father of Israel, a future great nation dwelling in its own land. Abraham saw himself as the father of a long line of descendants, and Matthew portrays Jesus as the ultimate son of Abraham in whom all God's promises will be fulfilled, and

b) a descendant (son) of David, who was the famous king of Israel's past glory. As a descendant of David, Jesus is shown to be both thoroughly Jewish and royal. It was through David's power, which was given by God, that Israel's God ensured the safety and prosperity of his people.

Jesus is portrayed by Matthew as a king, like David, and so he can be called Son of God, for God promised David in 2 Samuel 7:14 that David's son would be his son and that God would be his father. However Jesus' relationship to God is more special than this – he is not just an earthly ruler. Matthew's story shows Jesus as Son of God in a unique way. An angel comes to Joseph who addresses him as 'descendant of David' and tells him to accept Mary's pregnancy as due to the action of God (1:20–1) and this establishes the direct sonship of Jesus. Mary was Jesus' mother but he was conceived not by Joseph or any man but directly by the action of the Holy Spirit. In this way Matthew suggests that there is something unique about Jesus' sonship: he can be called 'Immanuel', 'God with us'.

Not every modern reader of the gospels can accept this story of a virgin birth. Bishop John Spong is one of many critics. In *Born of a Woman: A Bishop Re-thinks the Birth of Jesus* he rejects any literal understanding of the birth story maintaining that Mary was not a virgin as she was probably a victim of rape. He also contends that belief in the virgin birth has downgraded the importance of women in history and denied their sexuality. Spong may be right in his second comment about how the story of the virgin birth has been used, but his case for rejecting the virgin birth rests on his claim that the gospels are mainly '*midrash*'. He says:

> The way the Jewish tradition viewed and treated scripture was very clear. This method produced what was called *midrash*. *Midrash* represented efforts on the part of the rabbis to probe, tease and dissect the sacred story looking for hidden meanings, filling in blanks . . . . The gospels . . . are examples of Christian *midrash* . . . . There was nothing objective about the gospel tradition. They were not biographies. They were books designed to inspire faith. To force these narratives into the straightjacket of literal history is to violate their intention, their method, and their truth . . . .

Spong is right, as we shall see, in saying that the gospels do not simply provide a literal account. Each of the gospel writers colours his account with his own theology. *Midrash* is the written reflection by rabbis on particular texts of scripture and the gospels do not fit under this heading. The rabbis would learn, study and contemplate scripture, and *midrash* would be the result of their reflections. Jewish rabbis were interested in what happened historically; most of the OT books were meant to be historical accounts. Some of them, it is true, were written well after the events they describe and may have been built on an oral tradition, but a sense of history was central to Jewish teachers. Likewise the story of the birth of Jesus is intended to be a historical account with a theological gloss. It may be literally true or it may be literally false; it may be making a point about Jesus' unique status. However it cannot be explained away by describing it as *midrash* since it is not simply a commentary on a book of the Old Testament.

The wise men or Magi

Matthew uses the story of the wise men (2:1–12) as a subtle play on a Jesus who is the expected Jewish leader foretold in Numbers 24 but who is rejected by Israel and accepted by non-Jews. The original 'magus' from the East was the prophet Balaam who was summoned by the King of Moab to curse Israel. God, however, caused Balaam to bless rather than to curse and Balaam's prophecy includes the following:

> I see him, but not now; I behold him, but not near – a star shall come out of Jacob, and a sceptre shall rise out of Israel. (Numbers 24:17)

Matthew uses a star (2:1–2, 9–10) in his birth story and this would have indicated to the Jewish reader that now the above prophecy was fulfilled and the predicted ruler was born. It is easy today to forget the extent to which the Jewish reader of Matthew's gospel would have been familiar with the OT. Matthew's gospel cannot be properly understood without knowledge of the oblique references he constantly uses.

The magi read the stars as part of their religion and this sign in the natural world pointed to a king's birth, so they seek for the child. Herod's wise men read the Jewish scriptures which pointed to an heir to David being born in Bethlehem, but their reaction is different. Herod and his Council, although they are Jewish, are led by human pride and greed to be spiritually blind and not to recognize the coming of Jesus. In fact they go further and plot the child's death. Matthew is indicating that non-Jews are entering the kingdom of heaven through honouring Jesus while God's own people put themselves outside the kingdom. He is also showing that both the stars and the scriptures point to Jesus as the 'one who is to come'. Pagan religion is now overtaken by a Jewish Messiah who can be worshipped by all nations.

The life of Jesus is threatened and he is saved through an Egyptian refuge to which Mary and Joseph take him (2:13–14). This echoes the Book of Exodus where Moses is also a chosen child whose life is threatened and who survives through the action of Pharaoh's daughter. This is the second theme from the OT which Matthew uses in his story. Moses is presented in the first five books of the OT (which are called the *Pentateuch* and form the basis for the Jewish Law or Torah) as a crucially important figure – a lawyer, a general, a mediator and a prophet. Moses, therefore, sums up much of the origin of Jewish tradition. Matthew makes use of this background but turns the material round to show that Moses is still not as significant as Jesus. Moses' life points forward to Jesus, as the ultimate leader of the new Israel, and the signs at Jesus' birth re-echo themes from the story of Moses.

The adult life of Jesus

Jesus and Moses

The core of Jewish holy writ was the Torah (in Greek, the *Pentateuch*) or the first five books of the Bible which were attributed to Moses. The Torah provided absolute norms for all Jews of every opinion. After Jesus, the rabbis codified their interpretations in the Talmud and many *Midrashim*.

Matthew presents Jesus as the fulfilment of the sacred scriptures of Judaism and of the Law and the prophetic tradition. This is a major focus for Matthew's portrayal of Jesus' adult life. Chapters 5–7 describe Jesus as a teacher and an interpreter of Law. It is important to understand that these chapters echo the work of Moses. In Exodus, Leviticus, Numbers and Deuteronomy, Moses features as the great law-giver appointed by God. As Moses was given the Commandments by God, so Jesus performs a similar role, although the content is different. Jesus does not lay down a long list of laws but instead gives an interpretation of the laws that already existed. He cuts through the *letter* of the Law to arrive at the *spirit* that lies beneath the surface. Jesus focuses on generosity of spirit. It is not enough to be generous to friends and fellow citizens – it is necessary to be equally generous to one's enemies.

Instead of having to take tablets of stone from God's hands as Moses did, Jesus knows himself what has to be said. Moses brought the tablets of stone containing the Ten Commandments given by God down from a mountain (Exodus 19). Similarly Matthew portrays Jesus as teaching from a mountain (5:1). However Jesus is of greater significance as a source than Moses since he does not have to wait for God's intervention. Matthew shows Jesus as understanding the true significance of the Law from within his own heart so that he can validly explain it. Jesus' degree of intimacy with God is thus shown to be even greater than that of the great hero, Moses. However Jesus upholds true Judaism. Matthew sees Jesus' roots as firmly within the Jewish tradition, so Jesus can say:

> Do not think I have come to abolish the law and the prophets; I have come not to abolish but to fulfil them. (5:17)

Jesus, in Matthew's gospel, emphasizes the great demands he makes on people. It is:

- not enough to simply obey the letter of the Jewish Law, people have to be faithful to the spirit that underlies the Law, which is much more demanding;
- not enough not to commit murder, people should not even be angry;
- not enough not to commit adultery, people should not even think about it;
- not enough not to break vows, people should not make vows at all, simply being bound by 'Yes' or 'No';
- not enough not to demand 'an eye for an eye', people must exact no revenge at all;
- not enough to love your friends, people must love their enemies as well;
- not enough to give to charity, people must give in secret so that their gifts are not known;
- not enough to pray or fast, people must pray or fast sincerely and privately (5:17–6:18).

This teaching of Jesus is described by Matthew as The New Righteousness, as opposed to the old righteousness which the Pharisees teach their disciples (see 5:20). It is a discipline which is easy to take up since it does not involve all the detailed rules that the Pharisees considered necessary (see below). It has greater validity than the teachings of the Pharisees, since Jesus' teaching comes from God (11:29–30). Readers of the gospel are called to be faithful to this teaching so that they will be able to enter into God's kingdom, the kingdom of heaven (6:33).

Controversy and debate

Matthew establishes a picture of Jesus partly by showing how other people responded to him. Many of these figures are neutral or become his followers, but some are portrayed as consistent opponents of Jesus and his views. Key among these are those called by Matthew 'Pharisees'.

To some extent, Matthew's picture of the Pharisees fits with what we know about first-century Jewish groupings. In a difficult period, with resentment growing against Roman rule, the question of how God could be found at work in human history was more important than ever. There was no agreed solution, but one possibility was that God was held to be present to his people all the time, every day, when they remained faithful to the teachings of the sacred books. This appeared to be an attractive idea to many groups of Jews at this time (and today forms the basis of modern Rabbinic Judaism).

However agreement on this basic principle did not mean agreement as to how it worked out in practice. Certainly it appears that Jesus and the Pharisees had opposed interpretations of the approach to Law and how it should be applied. Matthew portrays Jesus' views as leading to generous forgiveness as a central principle, whereas the approach of the Pharisees is portrayed as leading to a narrow and ungenerous view of life.

Moses, in Deuteronomy 28, offers the people two ways of living – a way which leads to blessing and a way which leads to cursing. To the crowd in Matthew 5:1ff, Jesus is portrayed as offering blessing as opposed to cursing, presumably because they have chosen to go out of their way to look for God by seeking Jesus. Matthew here presents a challenge to his reader. Jesus emphasizes the distinctiveness of those who follow him: they will be insulted and persecuted (5:11), they will be like salt and a light to the world (5:13–16).

The theme of cursing is not absent from Matthew, but the cursing is reserved for those who appear to be following God's Law when in fact they are being unfaithful to the spirit that lies beneath it. Jesus replies to the Pharisees by saying that they themselves break the *meaning* underlying the Law by using one law as authority not to keep another. For instance, by making an offering of their possessions to sacred use they can avoid having to care for their parents, so setting aside one of the Ten Commandments. It is not possible to be certain as to whether this argument rests on Jesus' actual words, however it does maintain the line of argument put forward by the Matthean Jesus – that generosity of spirit is the central message of God's command and underpins the whole of the Jewish Law.

Ultimately the accusation against the Pharisees, as Matthew sees it, is that they fail to see God in Jesus and so reject God's kingdom. In 23:2–36 this comes to a head with the list of woes and curses which will come to the scribes and Pharisees. Here the other half of Moses' message bears fruit. People have already chosen their allegiances: those who choose Jesus are destined for blessing, those who reject him for cursing.

It is *most important* to recognize that Matthew's picture of the Pharisees maligns them. At their best, they would have fully recognized the importance of the spirit underlying the Torah. It is totally false to see Jews as a whole being obedient to 'rules' or 'Law' whilst Christians were obedient to the spirit. A number of the Pharisees would have recognized and accepted Jesus' message as set out in the previous section. It may be that after Jesus' death and after the destruction of the Jerusalem Temple in 70 AD all Jewish groups were forced to re-think their identity, and the community in which Matthew's gospel developed may have encountered growing opposition from local synagogues. This might have led Matthew to portray the Pharisees in a more negative light.

Jesus the teacher

Matthew has shown how closely Jesus can be compared with Moses. He also puts a great emphasis on Jesus' teaching – he is shown as a better interpreter of tradition than his contemporaries. As the son of David, Jesus carries out his rule largely through his teaching and interpretation of the Jewish Law. In the OT Solomon is portrayed as the supremely wise man and teacher; Jesus is that kind of person in the gospel of Matthew. Why did Matthew put such emphasis on Jesus as a teacher? The answer lies in his intended audience and their interests. Matthew wrote, as did all the writers in the NT, for a community of believers. He wished to make Jesus relevant to their interests and concerns in order to communicate his message effectively. This implies that Matthew's audience must have had a primary interest in matters of tradition and teaching. A clue here lies in 13:52. Speaking to his disciples, Jesus says:

> . . . every scribe who has been trained for the kingdom of heaven is like the master of a household who brings out of his treasure what is new and what is old.

This verse appears only in Matthew, and it comes as the climax of Jesus' teaching in this section. The content and position of this material indicates something of the Matthean community. They would have been happy to be described as 'teachers of the Law' (scribes) and would have understood what that title meant. This provides strong evidence that Matthew belonged to or was writing for a group of Jews who were faithful to Jewish traditions but who had their own interpretation of this tradition. As a community they were in conflict with other Jewish groups of their day who had competing views on how the past traditions should be related to contemporary needs. The 'woes' set out in chapter 23 are, for instance, a more developed indictment of the Pharisees than is found in either Mark or Luke. However both groups (Pharisees and the followers of Jesus) are said to have scribes so both would have been within the boundaries of pious Judaism in the first century.

Matthew's picture of Jesus as an adult fits into this picture. Jesus is seen as the supreme teacher whose authority equals that of Moses, the teacher of Jewish Law, and Solomon, the great and wise king whose knowledge was a wonder of the ancient world. In the Sermon on the Mount, Jesus carries on the work of Moses as a teacher of the Law whilst in the parables Jesus is more like Solomon, a wise man who uses observation of nature and the world around him to offer advice about God and the supernatural world. In both areas Jesus gives the reader a clear message which Matthew makes sure they will understand.

Miracles

Although Jesus performs miracles in Matthew's story, there is no special attention to these events except in so far as they are signs which reinforce the view that Jesus is an authoritative teacher whose interpretation of tradition is validated by God. The miracles of the feeding of the 4,000 and the 5,000 are inserted by Matthew in a section of text where the Pharisees seek the source of Jesus' authority to teach by continually scrutinizing what he is doing and asking for a sign that these are the result of God's work and not of demonic forces.

Mark and Matthew use miracles differently. Mark (as we shall see) uses healings and exorcisms to lead the reader to ask questions about who Jesus really is. It is an open question whether Jesus' power comes from God or the Devil (see p. 40). In Matthew, by contrast, the miracles are used to validate Jesus' authority as coming from God.

Fulfilment

Fulfilment of prophecy is a central theme for Matthew and reflects his concern to show how truly Jewish Jesus really is. In particular, the first chapters of this gospel directly refer to how Jesus' life fulfils OT prophecies:

- Jesus' birth fulfils Isaiah (Matthew 1:23);
- Jesus' flight to Egypt fulfils the prophet Hosea (Matthew 2:15);
- the death of the innocents fulfils Jeremiah (Matthew 2:17);
- the ministry of Jesus fulfils Isaiah (Matthew 4:14–16).

This reinforces the argument that Matthew wrote the story of Jesus for a Jewish group who saw Jesus totally in Jewish terms whilst at the same time having a different version of Judaism from their contemporaries. The evangelist's comments would only make sense to those with knowledge of, *and belief in*, the Hebrew scriptures.

Community

In each gospel Jesus has followers, including a core group of faithful disciples. However the way this group is described varies from gospel to gospel.

In Matthew there is a great sense of an ordered community lying behind the telling of Jesus' story. Jesus appoints twelve followers symbolizing the twelve tribes of ancient Israel. These men found the new Israel formed by followers of Jesus (chapter 10). In addition, Matthew's account of Peter's acknowledgement of Jesus as Messiah includes the speech where Jesus states that he will found his Church (*ekklesia*) on Peter's leadership (16:15–19). (See also pp. 183–5 and 226.) Matthew also includes instructions from Jesus as to how disputes in the new community are to be settled (18:15–20). This assumes the existence of an ordered community within which a disciple can be placed and from which one can be excluded.

Jesus and his followers have similarities to other groups of first-century Jews such as the Pharisees and the Qumran community. There is a strong sense of community identity associated with the ideas of righteousness and forgiveness. After Jesus' death this was to find expression in the formation of an early Christian Church – from within which, of course, Matthew was writing.

Only in Matthew's gospel does Jesus deliberately found a Church – in other words, a community with a leadership structure whose task it is to continue the work of Jesus by teaching and healing. This leadership is portrayed as having the authority from Jesus to offer God's forgiveness to all new members and to continue to scrutinize the lives of all the disciples of Jesus. This community is the authentic 'new Israel' which awaits the coming of its Lord as judge at the end of time (cf. 19:28 and Chapter 16).

Death

In Matthew's Passion story his two themes are woven together: the theme of a Jesus like Moses and the theme of a Jesus who is a king like David.

Son of David

The last scene of Jesus' ministry, before his final entry into Jerusalem, is a key passage in each of the gospels. Matthew places the healing of two blind men in this position. These men call Jesus

'Son of David' and 'Lord' and it is through using these titles that they regain their sight. Here the theme of a Jesus like David reappears in the story and is taken up immediately afterwards in the triumphant entry of Jesus into David's capital city, Jerusalem. The passage 21:5 is a direct reference to Zechariah 9:9:

Rejoice greatly, O daughter Zion! shout aloud, O daughter Jerusalem! Lo, your king comes to you; triumphant and victorious is he, humble and riding on a donkey.

When Jesus is portrayed by Matthew as entering Jerusalem with the crowds shouting 'Praise to David's Son!' he is emphasizing Jesus' direct fulfilment of the Zechariah prophecy in a manner that would have been instantly recognized by all Jews.

Sheep and goats

After his arrival in Jerusalem Jesus continues to teach, by sayings and parables, his view of God's kingdom. This teaching includes condemnation of other Jewish leaders who oppose him. Jesus cursing the fig tree (21:18–21); the parables of the two sons, the tenants in the vineyard and the wedding feast (21:28–22:14); as well as his replies to questions about paying taxes and rising from the dead (22:15–33) are brought to a head in the Great Commandment (22:37), requiring unconditional love of God and neighbour.

The whole theme of this section of Matthew's gospel is judgement. Jesus' fierce condemnation of the Pharisees and the teachers of the Law continues and is brought to a climax with the parable of the sheep and the goats (25:31–46). This is, in many ways, a remarkable parable because Jesus makes a distinction between the righteous who will gain eternal life and the cursed who will go to eternal punishment, not on the basis of what they *say* but of what they *do*. Both groups believe in God, but the goats fail to see God present in their fellow human beings. Similarly the Pharisees in the gospel have failed to see God present in the life and work of Christ.

The true followers of God will be known by their passionate

commitment to the weak, the marginalized and the vulnerable; and those who are cursed will be known by their neglect of these groups. It is not even as if Jesus says that those who follow him will be blessed and others will be cursed – the blessed are those who do God's work in the world. Each person has to make an absolute choice in life – it is an either/or decision and this choice and decision will determine whether they are reconciled with God or excluded from heaven. The implication is that the Jewish leaders are those who will be judged for their refusal to accept the authority of Jesus and his teaching.

Pilate

Jesus has opposed the Pharisees and now the Temple authorities react, as predicted in Jesus' recent teachings in the city. Jesus, before his arrest, says:

> You know that after two days the passover is coming, and the Son of Man will be handed over to be crucified. (26:2)

The next verse starts with 'Then the high priests and the elders met together', implying that Jesus knew what they would do even before they had met to consider it. They proceed to have Jesus arrested and killed.

Once again Matthew makes a subtle play between insider and outsider. Pilate (a Roman and therefore an outsider) agrees to the death of Jesus, but only reluctantly, placing responsibility back on the Jewish leaders and the crowds (the insiders). Moreover Pilate's wife (an outsider) declares Jesus to be just and a man of power (27:19). This is revealed to her through a common theme of pagan religion in the first century, a dream. In Matthew's story it is the leaders of Judaism (the insiders) who take the full blame for rejecting the true king and teacher of Israel. Whatever Matthew's motives for presenting the story in this way it has had an enormous impact in subsequent generations with these texts being used to justify massive oppression and persecution of Jews by Christians.

Death

Matthew, as well as Mark and Luke, include distinctive scenes in their accounts of Jesus' death: Simon of Cyrene is made to carry Jesus' cross (27:32); Jesus being offered wine and bitter herbs to drink (27:48 – possibly to fulfil Psalm 69:21); and Jesus' clothes being divided between the soldiers (27:35). The crowd mocks Jesus and, in particular:

> . . . the chief priests also, along with the scribes and elders, were mocking him, saying, 'He saved others; he cannot save himself. He is the King of Israel; let him come down from the cross now and we will believe in him. He trusts in God; let God deliver him now, if he wants to; for he said, "I am God's Son".' (27:41–3)

Matthew is once more emphasizing his constant theme: the failure of the 'insiders' to see who Jesus was. This, of course, points forward to Jesus' resurrection which then comes as confirmation of his status. Jesus' death is a moment of darkness for the whole of the world, it is a moment in which God is totally absent. In this culminating moment God's purposes are apparently defeated and those who oppose him appear victorious. The size of the calamity that has befallen the world is recognized by the Roman soldier who is moved to say 'Truly, this man was God's Son!' (27:54). Once again the 'outsider' sees what the 'insiders' had rejected. The death scene ends with a group of women left alone, watching the disaster – women, also, were 'outsiders' to much of Jewish religious life (cf. pp. 171–4).

Resurrection

The Temple authorities are so sure that Jesus is a fraud, and not the awaited Messiah, that they plan to stop his disciples from plotting to continue this false hope in Jesus as God's Son. They anticipate the claim of a resurrected Messiah and assume that this would be supported by an empty tomb. The only way the disciples could make this claim would be if they themselves stole the body away. The authorities therefore demand a guard on the tomb of Jesus to prevent this happening.

From a historical viewpoint, this is clearly something that makes sense. It is logically more probable that a body has been stolen than that a dead man has come back to life. As an objection to traditional Christian teaching, this theme has been raised in the twentieth century by H. Schonfield in his book *The Passover Plot*. As a committed Jew Schonfield may be influenced by his own viewpoint, and the argument which has to be constructed to allow for Jesus really appearing to die in the first place is complicated. However, the basic idea that claims to a risen Jesus were supported by fraudulent evidence is within the area of reasonable debate.

In Matthew's account, however, the story of the empty tomb is used to point in the opposite direction. The story is written rather in the mood of Psalm 2:1, 6 which says:

> Why do the nations conspire, and the peoples plot in vain? He who sits in the heavens laughs . . . saying 'I have set my king on Zion, my holy hill.'

God is portrayed as in charge of affairs. It is God's will that Jesus comes back to life, having passed through death, and appears again as a human being to prove the truth of all that he previously said and did. There is, therefore, some irony in the Matthean story of the plotting of the Jewish authorities. The truth is the resurrection of Jesus to life as the Son of God. Matthew points this out in two stages:

a) the resurrection of other human beings, possibly heroes from the past such as David himself or less important figures who had been faithful to God to their death (27:52);

b) the rising of Jesus himself on Easter morning (28:2–7).

The nature of Matthew's description, which includes clouds and earthquakes, is the way that the evangelist informs the reader that Jesus is exalted to divine status. Similar images are used in the OT in scenes where God appears to his people: where there is a theophany, a manifestation of the presence of God (cf. Exodus 19). Matthew and his readers would not have taken these as literal descriptions of events; they are conventional ways of pointing to the activity of God.

Against this God-centred interpretation of the empty tomb is balanced another, more human, version. This claims that the guards are paid to say that the disciples stole Jesus' body in the night in order to go on proclaiming their leader's power. As we shall see in Mark's gospel there are two possible interpretations available and the reader has to decide which one to take – although Matthew is in no doubt as to which is the correct version.

The climax of Matthew's gospel comes in the scene where the risen Jesus commands his followers:

All authority in heaven and on earth has been given to me. Go therefore and make disciples of all nations baptizing them in the name of the father, and of the Holy Spirit, and teaching them to obey everything that I have commanded you. (28:18–20)

Matthew's gospel begins with the genealogy, the list of descendants from Abraham and then David down to Joseph, and ends with Jesus' commission to his followers. Jesus' roots are firmly in God's people, Israel, but his coming opens God's message to all the peoples of the world. As the Jewish Messiah, Matthew portrays Jesus offering hope to the *whole* world through his disciples, who will be supported by the work of the Holy Spirit. Matthew portrays Jesus' life and death as the hinge of history: all past history leads up to fulfilment in Jesus' life and all future history opens out from his death and resurrection.

FOUR

The Gospel Story of Mark

Mark is the shortest of the three gospel accounts and contains no stories about the birth of Jesus. It is possible that the original form of the gospel did not have resurrection stories either, since a number of ancient manuscripts stop with the empty tomb scene. The passage 16:9–20 differs in vocabulary and style from the rest of the gospel and is not found in the earliest manuscripts. This appendix probably comes from a third-century editor of the text. It seems to draw on the Mary Magdalene story from the fourth gospel and the Emmaus story from Luke, presenting only a brief outline set of resurrection appearances. So the original version of the gospel may be even shorter than the text we currently have.

Mark begins with the idea of 'gospel':

The beginning of the good news of Jesus Christ, the Son of God.

This is nothing if not direct! To this is added a quotation from the Book of Isaiah about God's intention to come and save his people, having first sent a herald to announce his coming (Isaiah 40:3). This sets the scene for John the Baptist as the herald and Jesus as the king and they follow each other onto the scene in quick succession. Such speed of action is typical of Mark, which often uses the phrase 'And immediately' at the start of a new scene. This gives to the book a sense of urgency which the reader is meant to feel and respond to.

The adult life of Jesus

Mark moves swiftly into the adult life of Jesus and, more especially, into his public life. Verse 1:15 serves as the prologue by the editor and as a summary of Jesus' mission:

> The time is fulfilled, and the kingdom of God has come near; repent, and believe in the good news.

What follows is an account of Jesus and his actions and Mark indicates that it is in Jesus' ministry that the power of God comes to be realized in daily human life.

Miracles

Each evangelist shapes the stories about Jesus to suit his own story. Part of this shaping involves the order in which different texts are used. The very first thing that Jesus is portrayed as doing in his public ministry is to heal by exorcism. This forms a keynote for Mark's text. The entire first section is made up of a collection of healing stories. The dialogue at the synagogue at Capernaum sets the scene when an unclean spirit cries out:

> What have you to do with us, Jesus of Nazareth? Have you come to destroy us? I know who you are, the Holy One of God. (1:24)

The spirit knows Jesus' true identity as the man anointed by God whose task is to destroy the reign of the Devil over human beings. Jesus' audience is amazed and they recognize Jesus' teaching as being new and his power authentic because demons obey him. Mark's point is that the healing by Jesus is to be seen as the context for a new teaching. Jesus has power because God has delegated this power to him.

The effect of Mark's stress on the miracles of Jesus is an emphasis on Jesus as a charismatic figure, God's chosen servant, the Messiah.

In Psalm 72 the king is portrayed as one who cares for the well-being of his people and Jesus is portrayed in a similar way.

Controversy

As in Matthew's gospel, Jesus comes into conflict with other Jewish leaders. Mark recounts how the same problems of law-keeping and proper interpretation of the Jewish tradition arise, but here these issues are presented as of less importance than the miracle stories. Jesus' power is revealed in his healings but also in his forgiving sins, a power that, in Jewish tradition, was reserved for God alone. So when Mark attributes this power to Jesus he is making a very special claim, which is rejected by some (2:7).

Mark operates in a different way from Matthew. He does not lay stress on the details of Jewish Law and its interpretation so much as on the challenge to the source of Jesus' power. In Capernaum, the unclean spirit recognizes Jesus as God's Holy One and asks, 'Have you come to destroy us?' Jesus is presented as an agent of goodness, opposed to evil spiritual beings. Since Jesus' opponents could not reject the fact that healings had taken place, they attributed his power to the Devil and said that he himself was possessed by evil forces which allowed him to control other unclean spirits. Differences of opinion on the Jewish Law between Jesus and the Pharisees are also used by Mark to build up the picture of Jesus' opponents. They dismiss the claim that Jesus' acts are due to God because Jesus himself does not keep Jewish customs and cannot, therefore, be a truly religious person. Even Jesus' own family set out to carry out their family responsibilities by having him restrained because he was considered to be mad. Thus:

. . . and when his family heard it, they went out to restrain him, for people were saying, 'He has gone out of his mind.' (3:21)

Jesus' reply is logical. If his power comes from the Devil and if the Devil's power is being used to cast out devils then the Devil is working against himself, which would be absurd (3:22–7). Mark says that Jesus' mother and brothers come to seize him – a significant point as Church tradition holds that Jesus had no brothers. In order to preserve Mary's virginity the Church has had to claim (without textual evidence) that the brothers must have been from a former marriage by Joseph. In any case Jesus rejects his family and instead says that his real relatives are those who do God's will (3:34–5).

Parables

It is noticeable in Mark's gospel that material is gathered together by type. After the series of healings in chapters 1 and 2 come a series of controversies and then, in chapter 4, the focus switches to parables. Mark has few sayings of Jesus and mainly shows Jesus explaining God's teaching through parable stories.

The sower and the seed (4:1–8) is taken as a typical example and given extended coverage. Firstly Jesus tells the story to the crowd and then gives an interpretation to his disciples. As it stands, the parable has an open-ended meaning. The message, as Jesus interprets it, appears to be about the nature of faith and how faith can mature in a person and form a harvest of belief in God. Some people, however, will refuse faith completely and others will allow it to wither away.

Mark offers a further refinement. Jesus has made the parable – which by nature is open-ended – have a clear meaning. However this meaning is only for the inner group. For the rest it is as with the prophet Isaiah (Isaiah 6:9–10): God sends his servant to reveal his truth yet people will be prevented from understanding and thus be unable to find God. There is a deliberate re-use here of an OT prophetic passage. In both cases, Isaiah and Mark, the purpose is to deal with actual historical reality. It was a fact that not all those who heard Isaiah or Jesus accepted their message as coming from God, an explanation had to be given.

It appears that there is a choice:

a) either God cannot bring people to understand about him (in this case, God appears less than all-powerful),

b) or God chooses not to reveal himself to some people.

The first option is clearly an unacceptable answer, so this leaves both the writer of Isaiah and Mark no choice but to emphasize b). The problem is, however, that God must not appear to be tyrannical. This remains a mystery or, what could be worse, a problem for ideas about God. This is a forerunner of the long debate in Christian theology between the idea of predestination (the view that God predestines some for salvation and others for punishment) and freedom.

The problem is complicated by the mention in Mark 4:15 of the work of the Devil/Satan who blocks reception of God's message. However Mark prefers to leave the reader seeing God as finally in charge of events, even at the cost of attributing some arbitrariness to God's relationship to human beings:

> . . . but for those outside, everything comes in parables in order that they may indeed look, but not perceive; and may indeed listen, but not understand; so that they may not turn again and be forgiven. (4:11–12)

It is noteworthy that there is no idea here of human free will choosing not to hear God's message. If this had been the case the message could have been plain but it could have been rejected due, for instance, to the cost of taking it seriously. However Mark does not leave this option open – some who hear are prevented by God from understanding. The picture that emerges may be, to today's ears, of a capricious God who chooses who will and who will not understand. However Mark had no way out unless he was to limit God's power (as argued for in *The Puzzle of Evil* by Peter Vardy) and this he was unwilling to do.

The fact that Jesus' identity is not clearly disclosed plays on the idea of an enigmatic Messiah: now you see God in Jesus, now you don't. There is nothing obvious and, were it not for Mark's reference to God keeping the truth from people, each individual could be seen as having to decide whether or not to respond to Jesus. Human freedom would thus be preserved and individuals could choose to shut out Jesus' divinity.

Jesus has a mysterious aspect to his ministry. He heals but tells those whom he heals not to explain what has happened to them. He teaches, but tells his disciples that most people will not understand his message. This mysterious side of Jesus is emphasized by Mark's use of the phrase 'Son of Man'. Of course, the term 'Son of Man' appears more widely in the gospels than in Mark alone, but it is used by each evangelist to express a message about his own particular idea of Jesus. In Mark, the title is used as a way of emphasizing Jesus' enigmatic character. In a vital scene, Peter identifies Jesus specifically:

> On the way [Jesus] asked his disciples, 'Who do people say that I am?' And they answered him, 'John the Baptist; and others say Elijah; and still others one of the prophets.' He asked them, 'But who do you say that I am?' Peter answered him, 'You are the Messiah.' Then he sternly ordered them not to tell anyone about him. (8:27–30)

After Peter's proclamation Jesus replies by talking of how the Son of Man must die. In Mark's gospel, Jesus does not use the title of 'Messiah' about himself until his trial. By having Jesus describe his own work less directly, through the title 'Son of Man', Mark preserves the ambiguity in the figure of Jesus. He creates a gap between the visible healer and teacher and the invisible heavenly figure authorized to a kingship role by God. (cf. pp. 13–15.)

Mark's Jesus is a radical and harsh figure. His own family and their ties of kinship are rejected and he teaches his followers that they must give up family and social setting if they are indeed to be part of the kingdom of God. Following God is portrayed as incredibly demanding and all human relationships and worldly wealth must be put firmly into second place (10:17–31).

Jesus is just as radical when offering advice on the Jewish Law. Marriage is part of God's plan for human beings and no human being can interfere with a marriage made according to the Law's requirements. It is not enough, however, to keep the basic code of the Ten Commandments. All property must be given up and the disciple must put his trust in Jesus alone, separating from all normal ties of human society. There seems to be a tension between:

a) Jesus' view that marriage is a part of God's plan for the world, and
b) the call to put everything in second place to God.

Mark maintains both these positions and there need not be any incompatibility between them.

Jesus, as portrayed by Mark, can also be harsh in his relations with strangers. When he is approached by a Syro-Phoenician woman for help, Jesus at first replies that her problem is nothing to do with him and shrugs her off (7:27). (See also pp. 217–18.) He is only won round to healing her sick daughter by the woman's persistence. In this passage Jesus appears to be exclusive, implying that his message is only for the Jews. However in 9:38–41, when John is portrayed as coming to Jesus complaining that someone other than the disciples was driving out demons in Jesus' name, Jesus replies:

Do not stop him . . . whoever is not against us is for us.

The lack of exclusivism would have struck readers and is in marked contrast to the approach taken in John's gospel, where Jesus' followers are portrayed as a more exclusive group, or the approach taken by other Jewish groups at the time, when exclusivism seems to have been a common feature.

Death

Given this background, it is not surprising that Jesus' opponents wish to remove him from the scene. His harsh and uncompromising portrayal provokes one of two responses: either discipleship or rejection. Mark's Jesus confronts people with a choice, and given the tough portrayal of discipleship it is not surprising that many, including the Jewish leaders, choose to reject him.

The Passion account, like the rest of Jesus' ministry, is structured by Mark around two themes: recognition and rejection. Jesus is shown at the Last Supper as the Messiah of power, where he reveals to his disciples that he expects to eat a messianic banquet with them in the near future. However this power disappears when Jesus is arrested and tried by human authorities. At his trial by the Temple leaders Jesus claims for the first time that he is the Messiah:

> . . . the high priest asked him, 'Are you the Messiah, the Son of the Blessed One?' Jesus said, 'I am; and you will see the Son of man seated at the right hand of the Power, and coming with the clouds of heaven.' (14:61–2)

At last there is a clear statement of his identity, the 'secret' is a secret no longer. However the authorities claim that he is a blasphemer, a liar. It is not obvious to them that Jesus speaks the truth. Here again Mark plays on the ambiguity of Jesus. He is declared as the Messiah, the chosen one of God, the King; and yet he is helpless in the hands of the priests and the authorities. He is humiliated by the soldiers who mock his kingship and who see just a deluded figure.

The crucifixion story brings the faith and rejection themes together. Jesus' death scene is based on Psalm 22, the words from which Mark attributes to Jesus:

> My God, my God, why have you forsaken me? (Psalm 22:1; Mark 15:34)

The first part of Psalm 22 is a message of intense suffering and this is fulfilled in the death of Jesus. The second part of Psalm 22 turns to a hymn of triumph – the suffering one now knows joy and bliss. It is not quoted in Mark but first-century readers would have been familiar with this psalm. They would have known the OT and would have caught the implication. One of the problems with reading the gospels today is that allusions with which readers would have been familiar at the time of writing are familiar no longer and this can mean that the message and the point the writer is making become obscured.

As Jesus died on the cross, the crowd thinks that he calls on Elijah but they are totally out of touch and fail to see what is happening. Ironically, however, their mistake is a pointer to the truth, for Elijah did not die – he entered heaven in bodily form. Jesus now enters heaven and as he passes through the boundary between earth and heaven, symbolically the curtain hanging between the Temple Sanctuary (equivalent to heaven) and the courtyard (which symbolizes earth) is torn in two. Only the outsider recognizes what he has seen:

> Now when the centurion, who stood facing him, saw that in this way he breathed his last, he said, 'Truly, this man was God's Son!' (15:39)

Here Mark offers the reader two interpretations of the death of Jesus: belief and disbelief, respectively. It is up to the bystander to decide, just as it was up to Peter and for all those who heard Jesus to decide. Mark is, of course, making the implicit point that it is also up to his reader to decide: Who is Jesus after all? A malefactor and liar? A cheat and deceiver, as the bystanders at the cross believe? Or the Son of God?

Does the coming of Jesus now mean that God's power is released in history to defeat God's supernatural opponents and so restore true order to the universe, as has been implied by the evangelist in the healing ministry of Jesus? As we have seen in 1:24, the unclean spirit recognizes Jesus as the Holy One of God, but others see the work of Jesus as some trick of the evil spirits to ensnare human beings further or perhaps as just a deluded prophet. Mark's point is that this decision can only be made by each individual, which is why Jesus remains ambiguous throughout this gospel.

Empty tomb

The empty tomb story forms the last scene in Mark's gospel, at least if it is accepted that the original gospel ends at 16:8 and the remainder of this chapter is a later addition. The women go to the tomb but find no body. What does this mean? Is Jesus truly the Son of God, alive and well, or has some human group taken his body away? The idea of angel messengers supports the first alternative and suggests a joyful response, but the women's doubt and fear supports the second view, thus leaving the story open-ended and the ambiguity retained until the last.

Mark is clear, however, that the signs are there for those who are willing to see. Ultimately Mark is in no doubt at all. At the very beginning of his gospel, Jesus' identity was affirmed in the first verse. At his baptism, Jesus was consecrated to kingship by God: 'You are my Son, the Beloved; with you I am well pleased' God tells Jesus (1:11). God's power comes in spirit form to possess Jesus and enable him to fight demons. It is God's Holy Spirit at work in Jesus, not any evil spirit as the Jewish leaders have implied. However these affirmations still leave room for a free human response (subject to the problem of God's nature, already discussed).

If people see this truth, why is Jesus' identity hidden? The Jesus of Mark's story remains something of an enigma that challenges and confronts people. He demands a radical response which can be described as harsh – there is no room for half measures. The one who responds in faith needs to go the whole way with the Master. All other human links have to be given up and then the disciple will enter the kingdom of God together with the suffering but vindicated King of Israel.

FIVE

The Gospel Story of Luke

Luke was almost certain a Greek and was writing for a community centred in the Graeco-Roman culture of his time. The text itself appears to be modelled on the language and manner of expression of the Greek translation of the OT which is termed the *Septuagint*. Luke also has a more deliberate style than Matthew or Mark. His texts have proper prefaces in the style of the Graeco-Roman histories of his day such as in Josephus' book *Against Apion* or in the *Letter of Aristeas*.

A new dimension was added to Luke's presentation of Jesus once it was recognized that the gospel of Luke and the Acts of the Apostles are two volumes by the same hand. Jesus is set in a new time frame that moves from the old Israel to the 'new Israel' represented by the Christian Church. Jesus himself forms the crossing-point between these two worlds, between God's work in the past with Israel and in the future with the wider world. All ways lead up to him and all ways lead from him. For Luke, Jesus sums up God's plans across the whole of time.

Birth

The birth of Jesus in Luke's gospel focuses on the house of God in Jerusalem. Jesus is explained in relation to God's Temple and to the body of faithful worshippers connected to it. This is a theme which derived from the OT, in which Jerusalem is the same as Mt Zion or God's heavenly home. It is the place where God most clearly reveals his power at work in human life.

Luke sets Jesus into a broad context of the history and tradition of Israel. The story goes back before Jesus' own time to the old Israel, which is symbolized by John the Baptist and his parents, Elizabeth and Zechariah. Both John's birth and that of Jesus are set into a story which is very similar to OT stories and which sees God involved in the scenes of everyday life.

John the Baptist's birth is unusual in that his mother is elderly and beyond the menopause. Like the birth of Isaac in the OT (Genesis 18:9–15), God's intervention is needed for the child to be conceived. Elizabeth and Zechariah are representative of God's faithful people to whom good things (the child) come because of God's intervention. The most important covenant by God with the people of Israel was the covenant with Abraham (preceding, of course, the Mosaic covenant), and just as Isaac was a child of the 'father of faith' – Abraham – so John in the same tradition is a child of faith.

It is while Zechariah is on duty in the Temple that he sees God's angelic messenger, Gabriel. Again this would remind the first-century reader of scenes from the Old Testament such as the birth of Samson in Judges 13. This story turns on the awesome appearance and disappearance to heaven of a messenger of God, an angel, whose presence ensures that a child of special qualities will be born to lead Israel. In Luke's story, an angel comes to prepare the couple for the birth of a special child. God is, therefore, closely linked to the birth of John.

This link is paralleled but surpassed when it comes to Gabriel's announcement to Mary that she will have a child who, she is told, will be called God's Son. She will become pregnant not by the action of any man but by the action of God. Again there is an implicit OT reference, in this case to the story of Hagar, the slave 'wife' of Abraham who was sent into the wilderness. There is a close similarity between the words of the angel in that scene and the words of Gabriel to Mary:

Now you have conceived and shall bear a son and shall call him Ishmael . . . . (Genesis 16:11)

Now you will conceive in your womb and bear a son, and you will name him Jesus. (Luke 1:31)

Hagar in Genesis 16 knows that she has seen God; Mary, in Luke's gospel, meets the power of God at work in his messenger, Gabriel. Hagar's response is incredulity that she has met God and lived, whilst Luke portrays Mary's response as one of humble obedience.

Mary's song on her visit to Elizabeth contains, once again, a clear OT reference. Hannah uses the same phrases to celebrate her motherhood at God's hands in 1 Samuel:

My heart exults in the Lord; my strength is exalted in my God. My mouth derides my enemies, because I rejoice in my victory . . . . (1 Samuel 2:1ff)

This and the following verses are closely parallel to Mary's song:

My soul magnifies the Lord, and my spirit rejoices in God my Saviour, for he has looked with favour on the lowliness of his servant. . . . He has shown strength with his arm; he has scattered the proud in the thoughts of their hearts. . . . (Luke 1:46, 51)

When Jesus is born it is not wise men (as in Matthew) who come to see the child, but shepherds from the hillside. These figures symbolize 'outsiders' in religious terms – bound to their work, they cannot be free to join in normal religious practices and thus pious people would have regarded them as only being on the fringe of God's kingdom. However these 'outsiders' are open to the angelic revelation and want to go and see the son of David who has been born for them.

The shepherds reach the stable and enter in, honouring Jesus. By so doing they come into God's very presence and are 'outsiders' no more. This is a key Lukan theme. In Acts 1:8 Jesus tells his disciples that the message about salvation must be preached to the ends of the world so that all nations may be brought into the kingdom of God.

This is more important than the disciples' expectation that now a risen Jesus will restore the nation of Israel. From Jesus' birth, therefore, Luke is showing that God has sent his Son not just to 'insiders' but to 'outsiders' as well. The old 'them' and 'us' distinction in which Israel was God's chosen people has been abolished. Now the distinction is only between those who will be obedient to God and those who will not.

Luke offers a deeper understanding of the rite in which Jesus is brought to be offered to God in the Jerusalem Temple. The Song of Simeon (2:29–32) brings together two themes:

a) the Temple as God's earthly home, and
b) a new hope which spreads out from Judaism to all the world.

Simeon is another faithful person in the Old Testament tradition who has kept God's word and now, in God's own home, he meets God's chosen saviour. Jesus has come to his own home but from this home his message will be preached throughout the world. It is significant to remember that the Acts of the Apostles is the second volume of Luke's account in which Jesus' message is spread to the Gentile world, and this scene in the Temple can be seen as pointing forward to the apostolic movement.

In 2:41–2 Jesus once again visits the Temple, this time aged twelve. He has now 'come of age' in Jewish religious terms and so enters another stage in fulfilling his destiny. Staying behind after his parents have left Jesus now makes the Temple his home. This event is not surprising as his parents would have been with a large crowd of people and would have reasonably assumed Jesus was with other relatives. When his anxious parents find him he says that this is the obvious place he should be. Here Luke nudges the reader into seeing Jesus as the Son of God, chosen to carry out his Father's will:

'Why were you searching for me? Did you not know that I must be in my Father's house?' But they did not understand what he said to them. (2:49–50)

'. . . in my Father's house' can be translated '. . . about my Father's business', but the point is similar. Even Jesus' own parents did not understand his role so, Luke implies, it is not surprising that others do not understand as well.

Life

Luke shares with Matthew and Mark the stories of John the Baptist, Jesus' baptism and his temptation in the wilderness. In Mark's gospel only one verse refers to Jesus' temptation:

> . . . he was in the wilderness forty days, tempted by Satan. . . .
> (1:13)

In Luke as well as in Matthew, however, the temptation story is given in great detail. The Devil tempts Jesus in three ways:

• the Devil suggests that Jesus should turn stones to bread, symbolizing not just the ability to feed himself but also to feed a hungry world;
• Jesus is offered power and authority over all the kingdoms of the world;
• Jesus is offered the ability to draw people to him by using miraculous powers (Luke 4:1–13).

There are remarkable insights here into the human condition, as Dostoyevsky recognized in *The Brothers Karamazov* (pp. 288ff, Penguin ed.). The ability to feed people, to have political power in order to bring peace and equality, and the ability to ensure obedience have been the great objectives sought by people throughout the ages. Yet Jesus is portrayed in Matthew's and Luke's gospels as rejecting them all.

The first scene beyond the temptation story reveals the different interests of each of the gospel authors and is therefore particularly significant. In the case of Luke, this first scene shows Jesus reading a passage in the synagogue from the Book of Isaiah:

> The Spirit of the Lord is upon me, because he has anointed me to bring good news to the poor. He has sent me to proclaim release to the captives and recovery of sight to the blind, to let the oppressed go free, to proclaim the year of the Lord's favour. (4:18–19)

This message Luke applies to Jesus, whatever may have been the meaning and purpose of the original text in Isaiah. Jesus is portrayed as a servant and this points forward to his work with prisoners, the blind and the oppressed, and to his teaching and healing ministry on which he embarks in Galilee. This concern with the weak and the underprivileged is not unique to Jesus – it was a common theme of the OT prophets who had a strong commitment to justice, particularly for groups like orphans and widows.

It is significant, however, that in Luke's gospel the poor literally mean the poor – the word is used in a straightforward sense. Thus Luke records Jesus as saying:

> Blessed are you who are poor, for yours is the kingdom of God. (6:20)

It is this idea that has led many modern Christian writers to maintain that it is necessary for anyone who wants to follow Christ to take a preferential 'option for the poor'. In Matthew's gospel, by contrast, this wording is significantly changed:

> Blessed are the poor in spirit, for theirs is the kingdom of heaven. (5:3)

Matthew, therefore, alters the emphasis. This could be an indication that he was writing for a more affluent community who would not have liked the idea of Jesus singling out the literally poor as being blessed. Matthew's audience might have found it more congenial to identify with spiritual rather than material poverty.

Luke sums up the entire tradition about Jesus in a way which makes him a prophet as well as a king. Jesus will act as Messiah by bringing relief to human needs and in this way extend the kingly rule of God, taking power over demons and human opponents alike. Just like Elijah (1 Kings 17) and Elisha (2 Kings 4), Jesus raises a widow's son (Luke 7:11–17). He is therefore portrayed, like them, as a famous prophet of power. Jesus is shown as being compassionate to the weak and vulnerable, and with the power to give back life to the dead. Jesus is thus the paradigm of the prophet-king.

Outsiders

In Jesus' work, Luke focuses on his openness to the outsider, to the marginalized. In 7:1–9 Jesus not only heals the servant of a foreigner (a Roman centurion!) but wonders at the depth of faith such a foreigner, an outsider, can have. Later in the chapter, Jesus allows a sinful woman to touch him and to wash his feet with her tears, even though the touch of such a woman made him ritually defiled (7:36–49). Again Jesus rejects the 'outsider/insider' distinction.

Luke introduces controversy here. The Pharisees criticize Jesus' wisdom and leadership because of the latter event. It implies, after all, that Jesus is rejecting the Torah, the Jewish Law. Jesus, however, is proclaiming the spirit that underlies the Law rather than its letter, and he shows an openness to outsiders who are genuinely wanting to come closer to God. Luke frequently expresses this through stories about Jesus being happy to share his table-fellowship with many types of people, people with whom those who kept to the letter of the Law would never consider eating.

When Jesus sends out disciples as missionaries to proclaim God's kingdom (9:1–2), it is significant that he not only sends twelve to Israel – symbolically representing one for each of the tribes of Israel – but also a further seventy (10:1) – symbolically representing one for each of the foreign nations as were listed in the Tables of the Nations found in Genesis 10:2–31. Here Luke is projecting into his account of Jesus' work Israel's God as the God of all the nations of the world (and this is reflected in Genesis 1–11 in the OT). Jesus goes to Israel first but then to *all* God's people, completing God's work in creation. Non-Jews stand equal with Jews in God's eyes. This looks forward to the theme of the Acts of the Apostles in which Paul is portrayed as being commissioned by Jesus to go to the Gentile world and, at the Council of Jerusalem in *c.* 49 AD, the early Church agreed that Christians did not have to observe many Jewish laws. Luke sees Jesus breaking down the barriers that have existed in the past. With his coming all people have equal access to God.

Parables

Like Matthew, Luke contains more of the teaching of Jesus than does Mark. In particular, Luke appears to favour recounting parable stories. Some of these are common to the triple tradition of Matthew, Mark and Luke: the sower and the seed story (Luke 8:4–8; Matthew 13: 1–9; Mark 4:1–9) is one example. But Luke has other parables of his own which stress particularly the extent of God's mercy.

In the prodigal son parable (15:11–32) the reader is shown two brothers. The elder has been faithful to the father's commands all his life, whilst the younger has gone off and forgotten his origins until he 'comes to himself' and honestly resolves to return to base. The elder son resents the father's welcome of the younger son. Elsewhere, as in the dispute between the Pharisees and Jesus in 5:27–32, Luke shows how leaders of Judaism have disapproved of Jesus' open attitude to those on the fringes of the Jewish tradition. The father's speech to the elder son in the parable supports Luke's general line: The people of Israel are still important, they have always been God's people, but others who turn to God now matter just as much. The evangelist may well have been reflecting here on God's plans for Israel and the other nations. In Genesis 1–11 God is the creator of all the nations; ultimately all nations have their identity in the one, universal God. Luke is convinced that God is once more offering this identity through the work of Jesus.

Death

The union of 'insider' and 'outsider' which has run through Luke's gospel is continued in the Passion narrative. There are two themes:

1   The Jewish tradition is fulfilled in that at the Last Supper Jesus talks of the kingdom which will soon be fully inaugurated and how the disciples will feast in that kingdom (22:14ff). There are to be twelve rulers of the new Israel, corresponding to the twelve tribes, sitting on twelve thrones.

2   The cross is the ultimate symbol of the openness to the outsider – there was no more degrading death for a Jew (cf. Deut. 21:22–3 and Gal. 3:13) yet this is where Jesus is found. Through the cross a small group of faithful people will be the source of mission to the whole world.

Luke alone has the story of the repentant thief, who acknowledges his own sin and weakness which keeps him from God whilst at the same time treating Jesus both as king and intercessor. Jesus states that the thief will enter God's kingdom on the same day, and as he dies he takes the man with him. They enter the new kingdom of God together.

In his death, Jesus fulfils messianic themes. He has the authority to offer a place in God's kingdom to a sinner and, on the way to his death, to proclaim a message of judgement on the Jerusalem which has, through its leaders, rejected him (23:28–31). Ironically, the message placed on the cross, on the instructions of Pilate, tells the truth: 'This is the King of the Jews' (23:38).

At the end Jesus entrusts his case to the vindication of God by offering up a final prayer:

Father, into your hands I commend my spirit! (23:46)

The extreme anguish of Mark's presentation is lightened in Luke's gospel. Turmoil in the natural world is still portrayed, reflecting the disharmony caused by the execution of the Messiah of God, but Jesus himself remains a figure of hope and trust in God, in the midst of death and in an imperfect world.

Resurrection

In the final stage of the gospel Luke draws together themes relating to Jesus' life and work. On the one hand mythological language is used to impress on the reader that the empty tomb is the result of God's power at work (23:44–5); on the other hand the theme of Jesus fulfilling Jewish tradition is brought to a climax. On the road to Emmaus Jesus explains that all that has recently happened was destined to be since it had been written about in the OT. Jesus himself is not named in the OT; rather the key ideas found in the OT – such as kingship, prophecy, covenant and law – can be applied to Jesus to explain the deeper meaning of human life. Isaiah speaks of a suffering servant whom God will exalt. That, suggests Luke, is the best explanation for Jesus that can be offered.

The fact that the disciples on the road to Emmaus fail to recognize Jesus immediately reflects a human truth. This points to the fact that it takes interpretation to show that Jesus and Jewish tradition are connected. Thus Luke says:

> Then he said to them, 'Oh, how foolish you are, and how slow of heart to believe all that the prophets have declared! Was it not necessary that the Messiah should suffer these things and then enter into his glory? Then beginning with Moses and all the prophets, he interpreted to them the things about himself in all the scriptures. (24:25–7)

So Luke shows that although Jesus was not the Messiah the Jews were expecting, this reflected their failure to understand. Once the scriptures were properly explained, Jesus, as the fulfilment of the scriptures, would be clearly seen.

The culmination of the whole of Luke's message is the ascension of Jesus. This is recounted twice by Luke – once in Luke 24:51 and again in Acts 1 – and is told mythologically. It is worth being clear here on the meaning of the word 'mythological' in biblical scholarship. It does *not* mean fantasy or science fiction. It is used wherever God is described through metaphors drawn, for instance, from the term heaven – for example clouds, lightning, storm, fire, winds, etc. This is *the* defining language about God and human relationships in the OT and is the basis for much of the material in the NT where Jesus of Nazareth is shown to be one with God.

During the ascension Jesus is portrayed as going up into the clouds, but the significance of this has a much greater theological relevance than this one moment of time. Jesus is presented here as one who has a permanent place at the side of God, with access to all God's power. Jesus is, in this sense, part of divine power and represents a human channel of communication with an unseen God. In Acts, Jesus remains the means of access to God's power. It is by calling on the *name* of Jesus that disciples heal people, and it is in the *name* of Jesus that they found communities of faith by preaching and baptism. For instance:

> There is salvation in no one else, for there is no other name under heaven given among mortals by which we must be saved. (Acts 4:12)

Jesus has completed his task and now ascends to heaven. The disciples who were eye-witnesses to the crucifixion now understand its meaning and so they continue Jesus' ministry. A new stage in history is set to begin.

Finally, Luke returns to the theme at the start of his gospel. God will send his Spirit, as at Jesus' conception, to inaugurate a new age of history. In this new age, the good news of Jesus will finally reach all nations of the world, carried by disciples who act out the part played by Jesus himself. Close study of the work of Jesus in Luke and of Peter and Paul in Acts shows that the author deliberately relates the work of these figures to each other. There is a typical model of action consisting of teaching, preaching, healing and driving out evil beings. Moreover, in Acts 1 Jesus says that the disciples will receive the Holy Spirit, as he himself did in his own baptism (Luke 3:22), and will be his witnesses (Acts 1:8) by mirroring his image and showing that he is God's chosen servant.

While the disciples wait for this new revelation of God's power, the followers of Jesus are constantly in the Temple (Luke 24:53; Acts 2:46–7). This is at the centre of the universe and where they can fulfil their own true destiny as the worshipping congregation of Israel. They are still representative of the old Israel but very soon will become the foundation of the new Israel, in which faithful people of all nations have a share.

SIX

The Gospel Story of John

Structurally, John's gospel divides easily into four parts:

a) prologue
b) life of Jesus and signs
c) death and resurrection
d) epilogue

In the discussion below, these sections will be dealt with separately.

Prologue

The Word of God

Mark introduces Jesus through the use of the Old Testament (1:1–3); Matthew and Luke tell stories of Jesus' birth and infancy. John also introduces Jesus at the start of his gospel, albeit in a unique way. The first eighteen verses are called the Prologue since not only do they come at the beginning but they sum up the meaning of Jesus which is expanded throughout the rest of the book.

The Prologue was possibly written independently of John's gospel and adapted to fit the beginning of the book. The argument for the Prologue being separate is that its structure is very different from the remainder of chapter 1. The Prologue is closer to a hymn or poem whereas the rest of the chapter is a straightforward story. The Prologue has its own beginning, middle and end. It also has two parallel strands: the Logos (God's Word) and John the Baptist. The Logos plays no significant part in the rest of the gospel and, given the emphasis placed on the Logos in the Prologue, it would be expected that this theme would have been referred to in later chapters if the whole of John's gospel was a unity.

The core of the Prologue is that God is expressing himself through Jesus. There are strong echoes of the opening chapter of Genesis in which God creates everything by his Word of command. Each new act of creation begins:

Then God said, 'Let there be light. . . .'(Genesis 1:3)

And God said, 'Let there be a dome in the midst of the waters and earth.' (Genesis 1:6)

And God said, 'Let the waters . . .' (Genesis 1:9)

God is clearly operating through his creative word. It did not take long for Jewish scholars to make God's Word itself the focus of attention. For instance, Psalm 147:15 says:

He sends out his command to the earth; his word runs swiftly.

It seems possible that by the first century the Word of God had come to have an identity of its own, as one part of God's power. John therefore begins with the creative Word, which was also at work in creation, and next moves the activity of the Word on into history. In Exodus, God *speaks* through Moses to demand freedom for Israel from their slavery in Egypt as well as to curse Pharaoh for resisting his will. God's *word* comes to all the major prophets in the OT. Isaiah 6 and Jeremiah 1 both show God putting words into the prophet's mouth.

John introduces a further development in the Prologue: the Word of God actually takes *human form* and this incarnate power of God's Word is called God's Son (1:14). Up to this point the OT provides backing for John's ideas. In Sirach and the Book of Wisdom, Wisdom itself has this same ability to enter into human history and to dwell in a nation. However in both these books Wisdom returns to heaven. Wisdom is a disembodied power which enters history and then leaves it, to return again in another age. John, however, makes a new and special claim: only in Jesus Christ is God's Word revealed in its fullness. Only at this stage is God fully revealed to human sight and knowledge:

> And the Word became flesh and lived among us, and we have seen his glory, the glory as of a Father's Son, full of grace and truth. . . . No one has ever seen God. It is God the only Son, who is close to the Father's heart, who has made him known. (1:14, 18)

This claim moves John's gospel into deeper theological waters than is apparent in the other three. Something similar, however, is claimed in Hebrews 1:1–4, where the writer begins with a pre-existent, divine reality. It is important to be careful here. John, in the Prologue, does *not* say that the *human* Jesus was pre-existent; rather there is a divine quality which is eternal (represented by God's Word) and that quality becomes incarnate in Jesus. After the resurrection the human person, Jesus, has divine status but that is not quite the same statement as 'Jesus always existed'.

The human Jesus represented the pre-existent Word of God because of his divine status. Jesus is *both* human *and* divine, and it is the divine side of his nature that pre-existed before Jesus' birth. This distinction in Jesus' nature is important as it opens the way for a theological understanding of the two natures of Jesus, the one divine and the one human. John's account has led some theologians to see Jesus at the crucifixion dying with respect to his human nature but not with respect to his divine nature. This, however, moves the debate into questions of Christology which are beyond the scope of this book.

John's point in the Prologue is to concentrate his reader's attention, from the very beginning, on the inner significance of Jesus of Nazareth. Only God offers ultimate truth about the value of human people and human history. The Prologue is clearly a Jewish text because of its emphasis on the use of God's Word which is validated by the OT background. Greek influence obviously existed in the early Church, particularly in the Diaspora (those Jews who were living outside Palestine), but the Prologue cannot be seen as a Greek text. The debt of the Prologue to the OT is clear. It draws on the OT but replaces Moses, the great mediator between God and human beings in the past, and the Law Moses taught with Jesus and his works. As 1:17 says:

> The law indeed was given through Moses; grace and truth came through Jesus Christ.

John the Baptist

Since the aim of chapter 1 is to link Jesus intimately to God, it is significant that the second part of the chapter is devoted to another human being, John the Baptist. Assuming the Prologue was a separate document, it appears that reference to John the Baptist was inserted into the Prologue early on:

> There was a man sent from God, whose name was John. He came as a witness to testify to the light. . . . (1:6–7)

Due to this insertion, John's name appears before that of Jesus in the Prologue. This approach to John the Baptist is in line with the other three gospels, where he is special but not the ultimately special person. However John's treatment of this theme has some features unique to his account. John the Baptist is a major actor throughout the first chapter of John's gospel. He is portrayed as a witness. He speaks his own testimony and describes both his own role and also the role of the Messiah.

John the Baptist quite clearly knows that he is not the Christ and also that his task is to make the revelation of the actual Messiah possible. It is John baptizing crowds of people which provides the opportunity for Jesus to come to public knowledge. Not only does

John recognize and proclaim Jesus as Messiah, both before and after Jesus asks for baptism (1:26–7, 29–30, 34), but John points the first disciples in Jesus' direction (1:35–7). The evangelist therefore uses the figure of John the Baptist to focus attention on Jesus. The Prologue introduces Jesus as God's Word, and John the Baptist proclaims the human Jesus as 'the Lamb of God'. For John, more than any other evangelist, John the Baptist has a vital role as Jesus' herald, as God's messenger and as a witness to Jesus' true identity.

There may well have been a 'Johannine community' which had a high regard for John the Baptist. They may well have seen him as God's chosen servant to herald God's coming kingdom. However the text quickly moves to argue that John the Baptist is only a fore-runner; he is the one who bears witness to the light. If this Johannine community did not join the early community of Jesus' followers immediately, then the way the text is handled here could imply that it was used to bring the stories of the two leaders together and thus unite the communities. The significance placed on John the Baptist in John's gospel is considerable, but it could have been achieved by the insertion into an original story of text drawn from the community of John's followers.

Life of Jesus and signs

John 2:11 says that Jesus turning water into wine at the wedding feast in Cana was the first of Jesus' *signs*. It adds that by this means Jesus manifested his glory and his disciples believed. This gives a clear clue to the shape of the story of Jesus' life in John's gospel. Here Jesus works wonders, as he is described as doing in the other gospels, but John's message is not just that Jesus is a charismatic leader but that he achieves his effects through the power of divine love, which is the centre of his being.

In manifesting glory, Jesus is intimately linked with God. It is God, first, who has glory. This term is intended to describe the brilliance of God's appearance, clothed in rays of light, and also indicates the tremendous power and control of events which God has through his omniscience.

The New Testament emphasizes God's creation of the universe and his purposeful planning of events. In the third chapter of John's gospel the writer says:

> For God so loved the world that he gave his only son, so that everyone who believes in him may not perish but have eternal life. Indeed, God did not send the Son into the world to condemn the world, but in order that the world might be saved through him. . . . And this is the judgement, that the light has come into the world, and people loved darkness rather than light, because their deeds were evil. (3:16–17, 19)

It is in the life and work of Jesus that the world is offered the sight of God's glory. However, with hindsight, it appears that the world rejects God since it rejects Jesus as the presence of divine love in creation. The miracles of Jesus become, therefore, an extension of God's creative energy and a sign of Jesus' role as God's Son.

As in the other gospels, some attention is focused on how people respond to Jesus. Here, one group of people, the disciples, are privileged to see Jesus' glory and to believe in him as the Son of God. The disciples feature in all the gospels, but their reactions are recorded differently by the four gospel writers. In Mark, the disciples are often blind and foolish about the true nature of Jesus. In Matthew and Luke, although the disciples have to be taught to see the truth about Jesus, they are presented in a kinder light and are portrayed as having some insights about Jesus and God's kingdom. In John, by contrast, the disciples are intended to be the model for the reader of the gospel. They represent what amounts to the perfect response to Jesus' revelation of himself. They see the inner truth and they believe. John's gospel has a strong emphasis on truth (see pp. 190–1) and this comes to a final conclusion when Pilate shows himself unable to see the truth of who Jesus was.

It is possible that John may have used a source document which recorded miracles, but if he did then he moved the emphasis away from the events to their meaning. Jesus heals and exorcises demon spirits, but to accept these factual claims is not enough to make someone a believer. Signs are the starting point on the faith journey. They offer the reader a way to travel into a much deeper understanding of the significance of Jesus. A series of signs is offered and each sign is part of a scene which shows a character either moving towards belief or failing to believe.

A good example is that of the man born blind (John 9). At the surface level, this is an account of a healing like any other but it is used to explore people's reactions to Jesus. Jesus is the main actor moving in and out of the story, which tells of the journey towards or away from faith. The man who is cured gradually comes to the knowledge that Jesus is more than a healer and he ends by worshipping Jesus as a divine figure:

'Lord, I believe' and he worshipped him. (9:38)

On the other hand, the Jewish leaders witness the same sign but reject the journey to belief. They set out a number of objections to believing that Jesus was sent from God, and they end by denying even the tentative faith of the former blind man (9:40–1). John is being subtle here: the man was blind yet was able to see with the inner eye of truth, whilst the Jewish leaders could see but were spiritually blind by wilful choice. They are therefore guilty; their blindness is sinful whereas the natural blindness of the man can be healed and does not make him unclean or impure. This would have been a very provocative text for those who did not join the young Christian community.

Discourses

The members of the early Christian community were prepared to put absolute trust in their memories of Jesus. This absolute trust in Jesus led to further reflection on the meaning of him. And this further thinking is set out in the great discourses which are woven into the Book of Signs. These portray Jesus as making long speeches in which he explains his significance.

There is a similarity in the discourses as each of them portrays Jesus as the fulfilment of major themes of Jewish tradition. In addition, the opening phrase in each of the discourses is 'I am . . .' and this draws the reader's attention to who Jesus is. This is a common formula used in Jewish and pagan texts in the ancient world when a messenger reveals his identity. So in the OT Book of Tobit, for example, the angel says 'I am Raphael' as he reveals God's work to Tobit and Tobias. The 'One who is' is the Greek version of God's name in Exodus 3:14 ('I am who I am'). So the evangelist was drawing on formulae used to introduce divine messengers as well as OT ideas about God to draw a comparison between Jesus and God.

In a difficult passage in John 8, Jesus ends the debate about himself with the statement:

I tell you, before Abraham was, I am. (8:58)

This points back to the Prologue and the idea that Jesus is God's unique, eternal Word. Indeed, Jesus as God's Word was present at creation (1:3–4). This makes a clear link between Jesus and God which can be seen as expanded and enriched in Jesus' self-descriptions in the discourses when he says, 'I am . . . (Water, Bread, Life, Light, Shepherd, Gate).' Each of these descriptions is taken from the Jewish tradition.

Water This was an absolute but scarce necessity in Palestine and in Jewish tradition is the means of cleansing and purification. Living water in rivers, springs and wells becomes a symbol for life and health in Ezekiel 47 and is used as such in John 4:14 where Jesus talks of giving the woman by the well 'living water'.

Bread This source of nourishment from heaven is what God gave to the Israelites after they left slavery in Egypt and were in the desert (Numbers 11). It seems that by the first century this text has been interpreted by some Jews to mean that the Law given by God through Moses in the desert was the true bread which nourished the soul. In 6:35 this tradition is given a new understanding. Jesus is portrayed as the ultimate bread from heaven. When an individual meditates on the person of Jesus he or she feeds the inner self with God's own food.

Life   God alone has eternal life and Jesus, representing God, offers this eternal life to all believers. The story of the death and resurrection of Lazarus reveals that Jesus is *life* here and now. If anyone believes this, then he or she will share already in God's own life – a foretaste of what lies beyond the grave. (See the chapter on 'Eternal Life' in *The Puzzle of God* by Peter Vardy, where the significance of John's account of eternal life for contemporary philosophy of religion is explained.)

Light   God is the source of light, and light (sunlight) creates life in the world. OT visionaries such as Ezekiel and Daniel saw God in a blaze of light. When Moses came down from Sinai his face shone so much with God's reflected glory that people could not bear to look at him and he had to go veiled (Exodus 34:33–5). Jesus now appears as the bearer of this same light to the world. He brings God's life-giving rays into the darkness of the world. (The Prologue also emphasizes this same theme.)

Each of the discourses begins with a theme and then explores it through the words of Jesus. The story then returns to show that the best way to understand a deeper truth is to see how it points to the fact that Jesus of Nazareth is the means by which heavenly truth is brought to human beings. For instance:

> He said to them, 'You are from below. I am from above; you are of this world, I am not of this world. I told you that you would die in your sins, for you will die in your sins unless you believe that I am he.' (8:23–4)

To take another example, it is not the manna in the desert which prevents starvation that is the ultimate meaning in Exodus 16; it is not physical food but spiritual food that is needed. First-century Judaism thought that there was no deeper truth than the Law given by God to Moses on Mt Sinai, and obedience to these teachings was all that God wanted. John's gospel aims to show that it is *Jesus* that is the true nourishment from God. His sayings, teachings and life provide the spiritual food that is needed to reveal God's perspective on life and creation. The last part of John 6 implies a link between a real 'eating' of Jesus and eternal life (6:51–8). This part of the chapter is taken by scholars as evidence for early Christianity's focus on eucharistic meals.

The same problem occurs in John's gospel as in the other three – there is no way of knowing whether Jesus said any of the things attributed to him by John. It is certainly probable that the speeches reflect the teaching about Jesus which was accepted by the early Christian community, but whether these beliefs reflect Jesus' actual words or are put on Jesus' lips to represent what the community thought about Jesus is impossible to determine. It is highly unlikely that the words are recorded precisely, but it is possible that the thrust of the discourses was similar to the thrust of things that Jesus himself may have said. The discourses are offered to the reader as a way to true knowledge of God.

Worldview

John's gospel is clear that there are two opposing positions that can be held: belief and unbelief. The passage quoted above (3:16), refers to God sending his Son. God's Son, God's Word, becomes part of the world, but not everyone in the world will accept him. The Prologue makes this clear when it says:

> He was in the world, and the world came into being through him; yet the world did not know him. He came to what was his own, and his own people did not accept him. (1:10–11)

Again, in Jesus' long speech at the Last Supper the world is clearly portrayed as being opposed to him and his followers as it does not know Jesus and therefore rejects God:

> If the world hates you be aware that it hated me before it hated you. (15:18) . . . 'They hated me without a cause.' (15:25) They will put you out of the synagogues. Indeed, an hour is coming when those who kill you will think that by doing so they are offering worship to God. And they will do this because they have not known the Father or me. (16:2–3) In the world you face persecution. But take courage, I have conquered the world! (16:33)

The gospel is under no illusion: although it is in no doubt about Jesus' status, it is also clear that many people will reject Jesus, not believe in him and will bitterly oppose the new Christian movement. John portrays the world and God in dualistic terms; the world and God are opposed. If John's gospel is indeed dated later than the other three gospels, this dualism may well have emerged during the persecution faced by the early Church, when the whole world was seen to oppose Jesus' followers. The world is portrayed by John as the preserve of evil forces and it belongs to the Prince of Darkness. Jesus' followers have nothing in common with the world and must come out from it and hold fast to the new world represented by the community of believers in Jesus.

There is also the theme of faith and offence here, which will be dealt with in a later chapter (pp. 215–19).

Death and Resurrection

The message of John's gospel is one for all time. Jesus is eternally close to the Father and all the events of his life point towards this eternal truth. The real meaning of Jesus' life is most clearly revealed in the Passion story. This story is the culmination of Jesus' whole life and is called by John 'Jesus' hour'. 'Hour' here does not mean sixty minutes, but a short space of time which has crucial significance because of what happens within it. In John 12, the evangelist has Jesus saying about his death:

> Now my soul is troubled. And what should I say? – 'Father save me from this hour'? No, it is for this reason that I have come to this hour. Father, glorify your name. (12:27–8)

Jesus' death is the 'hour' when he brings his work to completion, showing God's love in and through his sacrifice. In this way Jesus brings honour and glory to God, and also is himself glorified. In other words, Jesus through his crucifixion receives the glory of a king. From these factors in the gospel biblical scholars have come to call John's Passion story the 'Book of Glory'.

Lazarus

The Book of Glory starts with the story of Lazarus' death and Jesus raising him to life. Jesus here reveals that he is master of life and death – the greatest sign of his closeness to God. In spite of this miracle, many reject even this sign and plotters start to gather to kill Jesus. The Lazarus story sets the mood and is continued in the story of Martha and Mary in Bethany, with Jesus being anointed (12:1–7). When people criticize Mary for pouring expensive ointment over his feet, Jesus says, 'You always have the poor with you, but you do not always have me' (12:8). Jesus is pointing forward to his death, a death he knows about in advance and expects.

The Johannine Jesus is different from the Jesus portrayed in the other gospels in that he knows of his impending doom. Jesus does not agonize in the garden of Gethsemane before his trial as he does in Luke:

> 'Father, if you are willing, remove this cup from me; yet not my will but yours be done.' . . . In his anguish he prayed more earnestly, and his sweat became like great drops of blood falling down on the ground. (Luke 22:42, 44)

Instead, in John's gospel Jesus *knows* and *wills* his own death as his moment of glory.

John's text introduces a new character at this point, the Beloved Disciple. This disciple is specifically identified six times in the gospel: at the Last Supper (13:23–6); at the cross when Jesus commends his mother to him (19:25–7); when Mary Magdalene tells of the empty tomb (20:2–10); in the boat after the resurrection (21:7); when, soon afterwards, the Beloved Disciple recognizes Jesus (21:20–3); and, finally, in the last but one sentence in the book when he is identified as the one on whose testimony the gospel is based. He is always close to Jesus, both physically and in terms of his belief, and he appears in the Judean scenes leading up to Jesus' arrest.

Christian tradition has equated this Beloved Disciple with the author of John's gospel. However the gospel itself does not specifically claim that the Beloved Disciple is the writer. Some scholars have suggested that Lazarus was the Beloved Disciple on the basis that Jesus had a special relationship with the Bethany circle and with the resurrected Lazarus. Others, however, argue that the Beloved Disciple is an abstract character who did not really exist but who represents all true believers. No one view has been proved and the identity of the Beloved Disciple is unknown. However the Beloved Disciple at the end of the gospel in some ways parallels John the Baptist at the beginning – neither are 'the light' nor 'the Word', but they point towards him.

The Last Supper

There is some confusion in the dating of the Last Supper among the four gospels. Matthew, Mark and Luke record Jesus eating a Passover meal before his death, which means that Jesus died on the Jewish Sabbath (Saturday). John makes the meal earlier so that Jesus dies on the eve of the Passover (Friday) and is buried before the Passover itself. Therefore in John's account, the last meal Jesus had with his disciples was not a Passover meal.

There are advantages and disadvantages to each approach. For

Jesus to eat a Passover meal and to die on the day of Passover high-lights his role as a sacrificial victim. His blood saves people from the wrath of God just as the Passover lamb did in the Exodus account when the Israelites put the blood of lambs on the doors of their houses:

> For the Lord will pass through to strike down the Egyptians; when he sees the blood on the lintel and on the two doorposts, the Lord will pass over that door and will not allow the destroyer to enter your houses to strike you down. (Exodus 12:23)

The lambs' blood saved the Israelites, so Jesus' blood can be portrayed as saving his followers.

Although John's account of Jesus' supper with his disciples does not portray it as a Passover meal, nevertheless John implies that Jesus is, indeed, the Pascal lamb. As an example, Jesus is recorded as dying at the very hour when the priests began the slaughter of the Passover lambs in the Temple (19:31).

In some ways the Synoptics' time frame is less likely than that of John's. The Passover was a solemn feast and Sabbath rules forbade any work on that day. Crucifying Jesus on the Sabbath seems very unlikely since it would have involved travel and dialogue by the Temple leaders, and they were described by the Synoptic writers as active and involved throughout the process of Jesus' trial and death. John's timetable seems more plausible since Jesus is dead and buried before the Passover started.

It is possible to reconcile the two different dates given for Jesus' death by suggesting that Jesus followed a different calendar to that of the Temple. The date given for Passover in Leviticus 23 is 'fifteenth Nissan'. That date would occur on different days depending on whether a solar or a lunar calendar was followed. A. Jaubert pointed out in 1965 that the Qumran community followed a different calendar from the Jerusalem Temple and used this evidence as a way of explaining the Last Supper issue. However there is no evidence that Jesus belonged to the Qumran community and it is probably more likely that either the Synoptic or the Johannine dating is mistaken.

The whole of the vitally important chapters 13 to 17 in John's gospel, when Jesus is recorded as saying so much over dinner, takes place during an ordinary meal before the feast of Passover. John's description of the Last Supper concentrates on the meal itself. There is no reference that Jesus said anything special about the meaning of this meal nor is he recorded as setting up any mechanism for his followers to continue his actions. This is particularly surprising as, if John's gospel is dated quite late (see pp. 145–6), the Eucharist or 'Lord's Supper' would have become well established and one would have expected any evangelist to record the words attributed to Jesus in the Eucharist. This has been used as evidence by some commentators for dating John's gospel much earlier than is generally suggested. The closest John comes to a reference to the Eucharist is in the feeding of the 5,000 and in 6:53, when Jesus says (early in his ministry) that people must eat his flesh and drink his blood.

John's gospel lays stress on a different aspect of the Last Supper, namely the washing of the disciples' feet by Jesus. This humble deed is intended as a prophetic act to indicate how Jesus' disciples are to behave. They are to love and serve each other. The same message appears in Jesus' conversation with Peter at the end of the gospel, when Jesus three times asks Peter whether he loves him. In each case Jesus tells him to care for his sheep. This idea of service and care matched with love is central to John's gospel.

For John, the idea of community is very important. Jesus' followers are sheep and he is the shepherd (10:7–18); they are little children cared for by God the Father. The members of the community have a new identity: they are children of God, and brothers and sisters of Jesus and of each other. Jesus' new command is that they should 'love one another' (13:34). The new community is separated out from earthly ties of family and society – the world has nothing to do with them. The world is in darkness and the new community of Jesus' friends belongs not to it but to God and his coming kingdom. Jesus lays down his life for his friends because of his love for them (15:13).

The cross

The climax of John's gospel, the moment for which Jesus is portrayed as coming into the world — 'Jesus' hour' — is his crucifixion. Although there are close similarities between John's Passion story and that told by the other gospels, John's story has its own slant. The most crucial point is that Jesus never appears as a victim at the mercy of his enemies — he is always in control. When he is arrested Jesus declares 'I am he' (18:5) and his opponents fall to the ground, overcome. At his trials, Jesus is portrayed as having total inner control. When struck by the guard he calmly points out the injustice of the blow (18:22–3). When dying on the cross, he carries out all that is required to complete the event before surrendering himself to death:

> When Jesus had received the wine, he said, 'It is finished'; then he bowed his head and gave up his spirit. (19:30)

In John, no one takes Jesus' life against his will — he freely gives it up.

The crucifixion scenes reveal Jesus as a man of power and authority, one suitable to be called by the title of king which is placed above the cross and which leads to a dispute between Pilate and the Jewish authorities (19:17–22). This reminds the reader of the debate between Pilate and Jesus. Jesus is not a mere slave, condemned to a painful death by a powerful master; he is a ruler of an unseen kingdom whose death is permitted in order to reveal the nature of that kingdom.

John's picture is of a divine Jesus in full control, who chooses to allow himself to be crucified. Jesus' final words from the cross show him having completed the task he was sent to undertake:

> It is finished. . . . (19:30)

This is very different from the final words from the cross in Luke's gospel, which imply calm acceptance:

> Father, into your hands I commend my spirit! (23:46)

and the radically human cry of dereliction which Matthew and Mark attribute to Jesus:

> My God, my God, why have you forsaken me? (Matthew 27:46)

Thus three different gospels provide three different pictures of the dying Jesus.

Jesus, John and Mary

The fourth evangelist also relates a scene not shared by the Synoptic gospels – the moment when Jesus entrusted his mother to the care of the Beloved Disciple. Although this can be read as the natural human reaction of a son for a mother, who now will have no male guardian, that is probably only the surface level.

The Beloved Disciple only appears in the Passion narrative and has been defined as a model of the 'faithful follower' of Jesus. Jesus' term for Mary – 'Woman' – is a strikingly stark and impersonal approach. Again, this may indicate that Mary is being seen as a paradigm. It has been suggested that Mary may stand as a symbol for the whole of the Johannine community. (Another early Christian text, The Shepherd of Hermas, also describes the Church as a female figure.) Thus, another level of meaning in this scene may be that the life of the disciples of Jesus will, in future, be the responsibility of each committed follower. Just as Jesus loved the community so each member of the community must love and care for each other (15:12).

Resurrection

John's gospel follows a similar line to the accounts given of the resurrection in the Synoptics, although John has his own elements.

In Mark's gospel, the women leave the tomb in fear and silence; in John, it is Peter and the Beloved Disciple who are first to the tomb and it is they who respond with faith. One might speculate as to whether the women were regarded as having too central a role in the Synoptics. It might have seemed more appropriate for the writer of John that Peter and the Beloved Disciple should have been on the scene first and that they should have shown faith rather than fear. What is clear is that it is difficult to harmonize the two accounts. Which account, if either, is nearer to what actually occurred is impossible to say.

John also introduces another scene which does not appear anywhere else. Mary is portrayed as weeping at the tomb and meeting Jesus. The stress is placed, however, on the inner meaning of the event. Jesus is alive, but he is now a divine person. He can no longer simply be related to as a man. Mary must not give him a hug (20:17–18), and there is no reference to Jesus eating with his disciples or walking on the road with them. The divinity of Jesus is clear as much in Jesus' resurrection state as it was in the Prologue to John's gospel.

Epilogue

John's gospel began with certainty and the final verse of chapter 20 ends with certainty. Chapter 21 seems to be an appendix added to the basic gospel at a later date. This chapter allows both Peter and the Beloved Disciple to have a pivotal role and it could be that this gospel serves the function of uniting two communities, one of which looked to Peter as a central figure. If Peter emerged as the leader of the fledgling Church, this could also have been an attempt to reinforce the authority of his position by placing him in a central position at the end of the gospel story.

PART 3

BACKGROUND AND ANALYTIC TOOLS

SEVEN

Analysing the Gospel Books

In Chapter 1 the point was made that, for a future generation, even unravelling the links between Sherlock Holmes and history might be difficult. Twentieth-century readers of the gospels are in much the same position with regard to these books. The present generation is not directly in touch with the first century AD and its citizens. It is not, then, a simple matter of reading the book and meeting the historical Jesus.

If a search is underway for the truth about the man, Jesus, it is necessary to investigate the gospel material in different ways. Each gospel writer has a different viewpoint (as was demonstrated in Part Two) and the same story can give different 'pictures'. Whilst Matthew, Mark and Luke's versions of Jesus' story are closer to each other than to John's there are in some cases, as we shall see, direct disagreements.

Just as scholars in later generations might make intensive study of the Holmes saga and produce different theories of what the texts signify, so also, in the Jesus story. There have been a number of works of scholarship which attempt to explain the real nature of the gospels, where they come from and in what ways modern readers should approach the texts. In this part of the book, different approaches to the gospel material will be explored and explained.

Who, when and where?

Who wrote the gospels?
The first questions that have to be asked when trying to sort out the real nature of a book are 'Who wrote it?', 'When was it written?'

and 'For whom was it written?' Books provide a way of communication for authors, who tailor their work to the needs and interests of their audiences. If one knows who is communicating and for whom the communication was intended, this will provide help in understanding the book's message.

It would appear, at first, to be an easy task to work out who wrote the gospels. They are, after all, declared as the work of Matthew, Mark, Luke and John. However a major difficulty arises here. How do we know that these men were the writers of the gospels? All we have are the titles – at no point within the gospels is this information corroborated. There is a further problem. Matthew, Mark, Luke and John have been identified as characters within the NT books themselves. Thus, Matthew was the former tax collector who became one of the disciples; Mark may have been the young man who fled at the arrest of Jesus and who is referred to by Paul as a co-worker for Christ; Luke may have been a Gentile doctor who was a companion of Paul, and also wrote the Acts of the Apostles; and John may have been the disciple whom Jesus loved (see p. 76) and into whose care Jesus committed his mother when he died. None of this is verifiable. The most that can be said is that this information has been handed down within the Christian tradition. The earliest reference to the four gospels by name was quoted by a fourth-century Christian historian called Eusebius as coming from the second-century bishop, Papias. However there is simply no surviving evidence outside the gospels for a clear indication of their authors.

What is clear is that by attributing the gospels to these four individuals, the early Church wished to emphasize the accuracy of the accounts. The emphasis is thus placed on the *eye-witness* value of the traditions. As an example, John's gospel says specifically:

This is the disciple who is testifying to these things and has written them, and we know that his testimony is true. (21:24)

When were the gospels written?

The destruction of the Temple in Jerusalem by the Roman army is of great importance in dating the gospels as the date of this event is known – 70 AD. The four gospels treat this event differently. Mark's gospel has very little detail, just a prophecy from Jesus that 'Not one stone will be left here upon another. . . .' (13:2) This can be taken to imply that his account was written before the destruction took place. Matthew and Luke both show more awareness of the detail of the destruction. Matthew includes the verse from Mark but adds additional material (Matthew 24:2–31); Luke does the same (21:6–28). This implies that both accounts were written soon after the destruction when the events were still a major factor in the lives of the Jewish communities. John has no reference at all to the destruction of the Temple, implying either that his gospel was written before the event took place or some time afterwards when the events would have been less important. Most scholars prefer the latter view and suggest a date around 90–100 AD.

Mark has for long been recognized as almost certainly the earliest of the gospels as Matthew and Luke both include almost all of Mark's gospel in their own. (See Chapter 11 for a fuller discussion.) The earliest reference to Mark's gospel by name is by Papias (140 AD), as quoted in Eusebius writing in the fourth century. The problem is that Eusebius was quoting an older authority, who says that Papias said:

> Mark, who had been the interpreter of Peter, wrote down accurately everything that he remembered, without however recording in order what was said or done by the Lord. For neither did he hear the Lord, nor did he follow him, but later attended Peter, who adapted his teaching to the needs of his hearers but had no intention of giving a connected account of the Lord's oracles. So then Mark made no mistake in writing down some things as he remembered them; for he made it his care not to omit anything of what he had heard or to set down any false statements therein.

Eusebius' account is not necessarily reliable. It is produced 300 years after Mark's gospel was written and we have no assurance that Papias was correct, let alone that what Papias said was correctly transmitted. Later writers tended to make Peter more responsible for this gospel and to diminish the importance of Mark. In Mark's gospel, Peter is always presented in a humble role and this may support Peter's part in the authorship. This also supports the retention of Mark by the early Church as a separate document when most of its material is included in two of the other gospels.

Overall, it seems fair to say that the gospels in the form we now have them came into existence between thirty and sixty years after Jesus' death. This is a short time and may imply greater reliability than is sometimes assumed. This period is well within the lifespan of many people who would have known Jesus and who would have been able to say if the accounts had been fabrications.

One dissenting voice from this generally accepted view must be mentioned as it today no longer receives the attention it deserves. This is the view of John Robinson, presented in his book *The Re-Dating of the New Testament* (1975). Robinson produces a carefully argued case to the effect that the gospels, including John, should be dated much earlier than most scholars accept. He suggests dates for most of the material prior to the fall of Jerusalem. Robinson's view, if accepted, would turn New Testament scholarship on its head. It has attracted few supporters, but the arguments against it are not overwhelming. Evidence in favour of this approach may be that found in very small fragments of manuscript, which appear to be from the gospels, discovered in one of the Qumran caves. They may have been written in a style in common use in first-century Palestine. This could imply an earlier date than hitherto accepted, but the evidence is not strong.

Where were the gospels written?

At first sight this may seem an odd question. Why should it matter where the gospels were written? However this does make a considerable difference as each evangelist set out to perform a distinctive task. All the evangelists wished to record the 'good news' of Jesus' life, death and resurrection, but they each had their own interests which partly depended on their target audience. After Jesus' death, stories about him were handed down within the early Christian communities. They preserved the stories and it was from within these early communities that the demand for a written text arose. The audience for each gospel mattered as the understanding of a Greek, city-based audience would be different from a Palestinian, Jewish audience.

Such Christian communities became established around the Roman world. The Acts of the Apostles records the establishment of some of the first of these communities in major towns such as Jerusalem, Rome, Athens, Corinth, Antioch, Ephesus, Laodicea, Alexandria and others. It may be that one or more of the gospels was either written for or widely used by a particular community. It has been suggested that Mark's gospel was particularly related to Rome and this claim may be justified by the connection with Peter. The book also has little detail on Palestine and so may have been written at some distance from it. Matthew's gospel is particularly associated with the Syrian church and Luke's may have been the gospel used by the churches established by Paul. However the early stories on which the gospels were based would have been of central concern to all the Christian communities and can be expected to have circulated widely.

What is a gospel?

Today, we have four complete gospel books, but did whoever wrote each gospel simply sit down and write the text or did he use other sources which may have been written or passed down by word of mouth? What we have in the gospels is the end-product of a period of development during which stories about Jesus would have circulated widely. These stories would have been accepted within the different communities.

The evangelists, presumably, were working with material which already had its own history. Each writer would have had to take the different stories about Jesus and put them within a framework; he would have had to put the stories into a particular order and link different aspects together. He would not have been an author in his own right, rather more an editor who brought together widely accepted material. Each editor, therefore, shaped the material in different ways and in Part Two of this book we have seen some of the consequences of this. A gospel, therefore, is not simply a historical account. It is intended to give a picture of the life and death of Jesus of Nazareth and to convey to readers important truths about him. It is a 'good news' story. However the gospels are not simple factual records of Jesus' day-to-day life. They are more complicated than that.

What is more, there was no such thing as copyright in the first century. They were many editions of, for instance, Matthew's gospel. Once there was a text, this text would have been copied and each time copies were made there may have been alterations, insertions or deletions. The version of each gospel found in modern bibles does not follow any one, single text. Instead it draws on different versions which have been brought together. We have few texts available today which are dated earlier than 500 years after Christ's death and in the intervening time there would have been many texts and many developments. To speak, therefore, of '*the* Gospel of X' is, from the viewpoint of a biblical scholar, misleading as there were many such gospels. We cannot be sure which was the original and how the original was influenced by the previous material.

What was the language of the original gospels?

It is not easy to be sure of the language in which the gospels were written. Jesus almost certainly spoke Aramaic, although recent archaeological evidence indicates that some Greek was spoken in

Palestine during Jesus' time. There would have been stories about Jesus in Aramaic and there may have been early accounts of Jesus' life written in Aramaic but at some stage these would have had to be translated.

The earliest available manuscripts are all in Greek, and if Jesus and his closest friends spoke Aramaic there would already have been a gap between what he may have said and the written account. Something is always lost in translation. Attempts have been made to recreate an original Aramaic version of the gospels to arrive at what Jesus actually said; however such attempts are based on speculation. Probably the early accounts of Jesus' life were passed on by word of mouth and were written down, sometimes in Aramaic and sometimes in Greek. There would have been a mixture of accounts and a mixture of translations. There were also no shorthand writers or dictation machines present to record accurately what Jesus said so some distortion would have been inevitable in the years before the gospels, as we know them, came to be written.

EIGHT

The Search for the Historical Jesus

Some accounts of Jesus put forward by modern writers start by assuming that Jesus fitted into a particular pattern of Jewish life in the first century, and then go on to interpret the gospel stories working from this assumption. The gospels refer to some of the first-century groupings so it is important to understand something of their nature and differences so that one can weigh the evidence put forward by such assumptions.

First-century Jewish groups

There were a number of significant groups and movements within Judaism in this period. **Samaritans** were not strictly part of Judaism at all. The mutual hatred of Jews and Samaritans began in the days of the first kingdom of Israel but became worse after the Babylonian exile (when a number of upper-class citizens were exiled to Babylon), and the subsequent resettlement of Judah. The Samaritans built a Temple at Mt Genazim and rejected worship at the Temple in Jerusalem. When the Jews returned to Jerusalem from exile and started to rebuild the Temple, the Samaritans opposed them. Further hostility between the two groups occurred after 200 BC when the Samaritans allowed their Temple to be dedicated to the Greek god Zeus Xenios.

Samaritans, like Jews, suffered at the hands of the Romans. In 36 AD a Samaritan leader gathered together a crowd at Mt Genazim and threatened to expose the holy vessels in the Temple. Pontius Pilate ordered their massacre and eventually protests to Rome by

Vitellius, the legate of Syria, led to Pilate's dismissal. Although both Jews and Samaritans worshipped the same God, the antipathy between the two groups was fierce.

The Jewish scholar Josephus, writing from Rome in the last quarter of the first century AD, described four main Jewish groups: Sadducees, Pharisees, Essenes and Zealots. He called them 'parties', although modern scholars prefer to describe them as wider movements. It is recognized today that it is too simplistic to say that there were four groupings: there were many different movements in first-century Palestine and the relationships are complex and confused. It is important to bear this in mind and to recognize that Josephus' four groupings are not clear-cut and distinct. They shared a common Jewish tradition – the importance of the Jewish Temple in Jerusalem, shared rules for conducting worship, rules for ritual purity, and the call to true faith – however each of the four movements developed different interpretations of these traditions.

Sadducees looked to the creation of a Jewish state centred on the Jerusalem Temple. Sadducees were known for their conservatism. They rejected the enduring validity of anything but the written rules in the first five books of the OT (in Greek, the *Pentateuch*). They also rejected the idea of an after-life or rewards and punishments. However they strongly affirmed free will and claimed that the outcome of events was due to human free decisions, not to fate. The Sadducees lived out rules found in the OT book Leviticus and saw no need for any significant changes in these rules.

Pharisees relied on a similar OT background. Pharisees believed in adapting the Jewish Law to meet new situations. In particular, they applied the ritual purity rules which had been used in the Temple to life in the ordinary domestic household. This was highly significant as when the Temple was destroyed by the Romans in 70 AD, the Pharisee movement was able to adapt because it did not rely on the Temple in the same way as the Sadducees. Because the Law and purity rituals were centred on each home, the Pharisee movement could prosper and provide continuity for the Jews.

Essenes   appeared in the second century before Jesus' birth at the time of the revolt by the Jews against the rule of the Selecid kings of Syria. There are traces of their origins and of this rebellion to be found in the books of 1 and 2 Maccabees. Like the Sadducees, Essenes looked to the Jerusalem Temple as a means of access to God, although they thought that the Temple of their day was impure. Much information has been gained about them from the discovery of a large number of texts at Qumran which have been the subject of close analysis in the last thirty years. Essenes were a more widely spread movement than the Sadducees or Pharisees and were made up of many smaller, tightly organized associations. It seems likely that more than one branch of Essenism existed in first-century Palestine.

Zealots   appeared in the first century as a guerrilla movement, which gathered together an unofficial Jewish army to resist Roman occupation by force. They had sympathizers amongst both Pharisees and Essenes and there was a short-lived alliance between these groups prior to the Jewish revolt in 67 AD. When the Roman army ruthlessly wiped out this revolt and destroyed Jerusalem and the Temple, most Zealots were killed in battle or executed after capture. Some preferred to commit suicide rather than to surrender in the final struggle for the fortress of Masada. Zealots were not a religious grouping. They were committed to action against the occupying power and could have been Pharisees, Sadducees or Essenes. One of Jesus' disciples, Simon, is described as a Zealot.

Seeing Jesus as . . .

Jesus is presented in the gospels as in competition with the Pharisees – he was clearly not 'one of them'. He was also not a Sadducee, as Sadducees were priests. Some modern scholars have suggested that Jesus was either an Essene or a Zealot.

'Jesus was an Essene'

The settlement of Kirbet Qumran overlooked the Dead Sea from the north-west, about eight miles south of Jericho. The Dead Sea Scrolls originated in this community and were discovered in 1947, well-preserved in jars. These scrolls have provided important new information on some parts of Jewish society before and around the time of Jesus.

The discovery of the Dead Sea Scrolls and the light these throw on the Qumran community has prompted some scholars to see Jesus as a member of that community. Barbara Thiering interprets Jesus in this way. In the Dead Sea Scrolls two figures stand out: the Teacher of Righteousness and the Wicked Priest. The Teacher of Righteousness did not found the community but was of central importance in shaping its rules at its commencement and in giving it a purpose. However his leadership led to rivalries. His chief rival was the Wicked Priest, who attempted to prevent the Teacher of Righteousness from proclaiming his views. The Wicked Priest chased him to his refuge and interrupted the Teacher of Righteousness and his followers whilst they were at worship. Further, the community had a 'rule book' and membership involved total commitment. The task of members was to worship and study, although they also grew their own food. Three priests and twelve lay people were the leaders and there was a rigid order maintained with heavy penalties for anyone who broke the rules. As one example, foolish laughter earned thirty days' penance.

The obvious suggestion is that Jesus may have been the Teacher of Righteousness and, therefore, that the Qumran community and its scrolls can tell us a great deal about the *real* Jesus. Clearly if Jesus did belong to this community a completely new light would be thrown on the gospels, and it is not surprising that identification of Jesus with the Teacher of Righteousness attracted much publicity. However this theory does not stand up to critical examination for various reasons. Firstly, there is nothing in the gospels themselves to connect Jesus with this community other than the contacts that would be expected from a common Jewish heritage which was grounded in the Old Testament. Secondly, the whole pattern of the life of Jesus in the gospels – whereby he had no fixed base and resisted a legalism which defined holiness in terms of adherence to fixed rules – goes against the essential approach of the Qumran community. Thirdly, and even more significant however, is the fact that the documents of the Qumran community have been dated earlier than the time of Jesus. The Qumran community was established about 150 BC and was probably destroyed in about 68 AD, around the time when Jerusalem and the Temple were destroyed by the Romans. However the Teacher of Righteousness lived at the beginning of the community's history, in other words about 150 years before Jesus was born. It simply is not possible that Jesus could have been this Teacher.

Having said this, the Qumran community is of great importance for understanding Jesus. The Qumran community separated themselves from the towns and cities of Israel and went into the wilderness. They were prompted to do so by the text from Isaiah which is also used in the gospels to introduce John the Baptist:

In the wilderness prepare the way of the Lord, make straight in the desert a highway for our God. (Isaiah 40:3)

They saw 'preparing the way' as involving purity and enquiry into the scriptures (Community Rule 8:15–16). The Essenes at Qumran applied the ritual washing and purity rules, which in the OT had applied only to priests, to all community members. However they kept themselves separate.

If there is any connection between the gospels and the Qumran community it may be that John the Baptist could have been associated with it. He is portrayed as coming from the desert to deliver his message. Like them, he lived in the desert and was clothed in camel hair (common among nomads). But these are tenuous connections. John's call to repentance was addressed to all people and they were sent back to their day-to-day lives. John also substituted a single baptism by water for the daily bathings at Qumran.

Jesus went even further than John as he not only preached to everyone but he also mixed with them, lived with them, and ate and drank with them – so much so that he was called a wine drinker and a glutton (Matthew 11:18–19). The Essenes separated themselves; Jesus involved himself with and in the world. This obviously brought him into conflict with those who saw 'being religious' as necessarily involving separation and ritual. The Dead Sea Scrolls are vitally important in telling us about the Qumran community and, therefore, about the beliefs of one sect in Judaism at the time, but they do not really tell us anything about Jesus.

'Jesus was a Zealot'

R.F. Brandon concentrates on the claim that Jesus was hailed as the Messiah by his followers, and sees him as a Zealot. Jesus was a revolutionary – someone who had led a grassroots movement with the hope that through this movement a new historical Israel would come into being. In Josephus' writings (*Jewish Wars* and *Antiquities*) there are accounts of other revolutionary and prophetic figures who claimed, for instance, to be a new Moses. They led peasant armies to cross the river Jordan (which they saw as being equivalent to the Red Sea) and to approach Jerusalem, confident that it would open before them through divine aid. These revolutionaries were routed by Roman troops and their leaders crucified as a sign to all that Rome was firmly in control.

It has been suggested that one reason for Judas Iscariot's betrayal of Jesus was that he became disappointed when he realized that Jesus was not the sort of Messiah who would lead the Jews against the Romans. It cannot have been easy living under an oppressive power and many Jews would have hoped for liberation. The idea that Jesus was a revolutionary who 'went pacifist' fits the atmosphere portrayed by Josephus and has clear connections with events in first-century Palestine. However there is no evidence for this from the gospels or other NT sources. Most scholars, therefore, reject Brandon's approach as they consider it brings an assumption to bear on the text which cannot be justified and, in the face of the evidence, looks unlikely.

'Jesus was a misguided Jew'

The historian A.N. Wilson, in his book *Jesus*, starts by rejecting belief in God. He therefore sees Jesus as an entirely human figure, a misguided Jew. Wilson maintains that Jesus was crucified, died – and stayed dead. Probably his disciples returned to Galilee where they buried him. However Jesus' brother, James, reassured Jesus' followers that everything had happened according to the Jewish scriptures. James was considered to be Jesus risen from the dead, thus the myth (by which Wilson means the false story) about the resurrection began. James had not been well-known to the disciples, hence he was not recognized. It was only later that Jesus' disciples came to believe that James was Jesus risen from the dead. Proof of this theory is said to lie in Luke 24:

> . . . two of them were going to a village called Emmaus . . . and talking with each other about all these things that had happened . . . Jesus himself came near and went with them, but their eyes were kept from recognizing him . . . And he said to them, Oh how foolish you are, and how slow of heart to believe all that the prophets have declared! Was it not necessary that the Messiah should suffer these things and then enter into his glory? And beginning with Moses and all the prophets, he interpreted to them the things about himself in all the scriptures . . . When he was at the table with them, he took bread, blessed and broke it, and gave it to them. And their eyes were opened and they recognized him; and he vanished from their sight. They said to each other, 'Were not our hearts burning within us while he was talking to us on the road, while he opened the scriptures to us?' (24:13–16, 25–7, 30–2)

Jesus' followers, Wilson maintains, would have recognized Jesus but not James – at least not immediately.

In Wilson's view the real founder of Christianity was Paul. Paul so influenced the writers of the Synoptic gospels that they wrote accounts which made it appear that Jesus was the Messianic figure.

According to Wilson, Jesus thought of himself as a holy man, certainly not as the Son of God. He preached a simplified form of Judaism, stripped of the additions that had been laid over it.

Wilson's account seems implausible, particularly as the evidence for it is restricted to a very few gospel passages whilst other passages strongly oppose his interpretation. Paul, writing soon after Jesus' death (and much earlier than the date of the gospel accounts), wrote:

> For I handed to you as of first importance what I in turn had received; that Christ died for our sins in accordance with the scriptures, and that he was buried and that he was raised on the third day in accordance with the scriptures, and that he appeared to Cephas, then to the twelve. Then he appeared to more than five hundred brothers and sisters at one time, most of whom are still alive, though some have died. Then he appeared to James, then to all the apostles. Last of all, as to one untimely born, he appeared also to me. (1 Corinthians 15:3–8)

If the 'resurrected Jesus' was James, then it seems more than odd that his closest friends did not recognize the difference and that James managed to appear to himself. There sometimes comes a point when reinterpretations of the tradition are more incredible than the tradition itself. The above, of course, is no proof, but one is compelled to balance probabilities.

Seeking the historical Jesus

As with so many aspects of the gospel study, we have only the existing gospel literature from which to work. It is not possible to situate Jesus the Jew in any way except by looking at the historical background material in the gospel books and then trying to read back from that to the real man. This opens the way for much scholarly debate. What follows are some of the key players in that debate and their views.

Albert Schweitzer

In 1906 Albert Schweitzer produced his work *The Quest for the Historical Jesus* and outlined what he considered to be Jesus' understanding of his own work. Schweitzer based his ideas particularly on Mark 13 and Matthew 10. He felt that it was possible to trace the historical Jesus in the present texts, but only by accepting some of the concepts of the first-century world, in particular the idea of the imminent 'end of time'. Schweitzer maintained that Jesus considered that the end of the world and the new kingdom of God would come at the end of the year's harvest. For instance, Matthew 10:23 says:

> When they persecute you in one town, flee to the next; for truly, I tell you, you will not have gone through all the towns of Israel before the Son of man comes.

The implication here seems clear: Jesus expected the end of the world to come very soon. Schweitzer therefore considered that Jesus was one in a long line of people who have claimed to see the end of history – he was an 'eschatological visionary'. He was prepared to face suffering and even death because of the passion of his convictions, but he finally died deluded, forsaken by the God in whom he believed.

If this is valid, then it provides a way of selecting the real sayings of Jesus from later additions. Prophecies of the end of the world or claims of Jesus' unique position may well go back to what Jesus himself thought, but other stories and stories about miracles were probably added by later followers who wished to base a new movement on his life once he had died. The problem in this approach is obvious: it all depends on whether the passages Schweitzer selected were the central points on which an understanding of Jesus should be built. Reject this interpretation and Schweitzer's interpretation can be rejected as well.

As a contrast, later form critics (see Chapter 10) considered that Jesus' own views had no prominent place in the gospels. Perhaps there was a central core formed by a historical figure, but this had been added to and developed over a number of years and the gospels represented these stages of growth. It was necessary to strip away the additions to try to get back to the base material. Each separate scene could be examined in detail and explanations and expansions deleted in order to arrive at the core. On this basis, no clear picture of the historical Jesus can be recovered. Rudolf Bultmann took this view.

Ruldolf Bultmann

The most famous of all form critics was Rudolf Bultmann, whose two most important books were *The History of the Synoptic Tradition* (1921) and *The Gospel of John* (1941). Bultmann dominated New Testament scholarship for fifty years and firmly rejected Albert Schweitzer's *Quest*. He not only worked on the classification of different types of literature but passed judgement on the question of historicity of the gospel records.

Bultmann saw clearly the difficulty in moving back from the text to the 'historical' Jesus and came to the conclusion that the stories in the gospels about Jesus owed more to the imagination of the early Christian writers than they do to the recording of historical events. He claimed that the gospels express the *meaning* of Jesus in the religious language of first-century times. He was at pains to 'decode' that language so that the message of the evangelist would be transmitted to a twentieth-century audience.

Since much of the New Testament was written in metaphorical language and drew on first-century Jewish mythology (for instance, the description of God as coming in clouds), this decoding turned into 'demythologizing' of the text. For Bultmann, the gospels are a myth (see pp. 57–8 for a definition of myth: it does *not* mean a fictional story; myths could express truths), although he did accept the crucifixion as a historical event. Whilst he did not actually deny that Jesus existed as a historical person, he claimed that our knowledge of Jesus is so limited that the historical Jesus was of no significance. Bultmann maintained that the gospels merely reflected what Christians in the first century thought about Jesus rather than what actually occurred.

John's gospel makes clear, as we have seen, that God's Word became incarnate at a particular moment in human history. Bultmann, however, denies this and claims that it is only when Christianity is preached that God's Word actually enters the world of history in which human beings live. Bultmann dismissed any search for historical truth as irrelevant: the gospel stories contain some minimal truths but what is important is the preaching which is based on these stories. As one example, the extract below is an often-quoted rejection by Bultmann of the idea that the modern reader can take seriously the gospel ideas in the form they have been transmitted to us:

> . . . it is impossible to use electric light and the wireless and to avail oneself of modern medical and surgical discoveries, and at the same time to believe in the New Testament world of Daemons and Spirits. (*Kerygma and Myth: A Theological Debate*, ed. H. Bartsch, p. 5)

If the stories about Jesus can be separated from any claim to historicity, they can be re-expressed in ways which are influenced by contemporary thinking and which may be held, therefore, to be more relevant to today's world. As an example, the resurrection stories could be seen as a way of people expressing their feeling of the ongoing relevance of Jesus' message or their feeling that Jesus' spirit is still alive even though he has in fact died. On this basis, the stories could be looked on as owing a great deal to human psychology instead of to historical fact. Hence, Jesus did not rise from the dead, but stories about him were told to explain why he was still relevant to people who followed him.

The 'New Quest' scholars

The original quest for the historical Jesus was the work of liberal Protestant scholars of the late nineteenth and early twentieth centuries (such as Reimarus). This investigation of the gospels assumed that it would be easy to find traces of the original Jesus hidden in the text. This Jesus was a simple teacher and healer, a very human figure whose image had, it was assumed, been later turned into a supernatural, divine being.

This quest was undermined by the research on texts which showed how complex the development of the gospel tradition was and how the present gospels were the result of many years of Christian reflection on the significance of Jesus. The work of Bultmann, in particular, highlighted the difficulties. However Bultmann's ideas were, in turn, superceded by a new initiative.

This search is different from the first one in that it accepts that it is impossible to reach back to a human being, Jesus of Nazareth, in any simple way. The gospels describe a Christ figure, a saviour, rather than a historical character. However, it is argued, the evangelists have not invented this kind of Jesus figure of their own accord. The gospels are in touch with the first-century experience of the historical Jesus. If the Jesus of the gospels talked about the 'end of time', the historical Jesus also discussed these subjects. He did this with authority, an authority which was impressive even in his lifetime. The picture given in the gospels of a Christ who is the universal saviour is held to be an expression of the impact Jesus himself made.

The title 'New Quest' is derived from the work of J.M. Robinson, whose book, *A New Quest for the Historical Jesus* was published in 1959. The book title gave rise to the term by which a whole movement of scholarship was known. The New Quest scholars argued, in different ways, that the gospels *do* provide access to the historical Jesus. G. Bornkamm (*Jesus of Nazareth*, 1956), like two earlier scholars Käsemann and Fuchs, maintained that the picture of Jesus in the gospels was not one manufactured by the early Christians – a product of their faith – but was a faithfully preserved memory of the actual man. Bornkamm also argued that many of the basic, neutral facts about Jesus' background come through in the gospel stories. These include the name of his foster father, Joseph, and his village, Nazareth of Galilee. It is thus possible, Bornkamm held, to put together a fairly precise account of the outlines of the career of Jesus from the gospel books.

H. Conzelmann was another scholar in the New Quest school. He stressed the fact that it is in and through history that God is made known. Conzelmann focused on Luke and maintained that Luke's gospel provided an account of how the whole of history serves God's purposes to make known God's nature and establish God's control over the whole world. Luke sees Jesus as the culmination of the 'old Israel' – he is the child of a generation of faithful Jews who constantly look for God's intervention in history. Jesus' life forms the 'hinge' of all time, for he *is* the divine intervention in history. After Jesus' ascension the life of the 'New Israel' flows out from Jerusalem in the work of the missionary activity of the early disciples.

Finally, J.M. Robinson himself addressed the issue of Jesus and history through the approach to history created by the historians Dilthey and Collingwood. Once again, the idea was to show that God can be known through human history. Jesus was a human being but one who focused God's activity in time and space. It is not foolishness to think of Jesus both as the carpenter's son and also as God's Son because it is part of the very nature of historical truth that it can make God's presence known.

Since the New Quest movement of the 1950s and 1960s, a good deal more information has become available to scholars, notably from the Qumran texts. It is now easier to accept the historical reality of Jesus the Jew in first-century Palestine. However the approach to history on which the New Quest movement was founded has been superceded by new philosophies of history. The New Quest movement is now as much a matter of the history of biblical scholarship as was Bultmann's scepticism.

E.P. Sanders and others

More modern scholars have also opposed Bultmann's views. E.P. Sanders claims in *The Historical Figure of Jesus* (Penguin, 1994) that:

> We know a lot about Jesus . . . vastly more than about . . . any of the other figures whose names we have from his time and place.

[Preface] We have a good idea of the main lines of his ministry and message. We know who he was, what he did, what he taught and why he died . . . we know how much he inspired his followers. [Epilogue]

In his earlier book. *Jesus and Judaism* (1985) Sanders argued that Jesus was not only a Jew but always intended to remain within Judaism. He had no intention at all of setting up a new movement and it was his followers who broke away from mainstream Judaism. Jews, at the time of Jesus, considered healing to be a religious practice and Jesus was renowned for the cures he effected. These cures gave authority to his religious teaching. Sanders rejects any idea that Jesus saw himself as a Messianic figure, although Jesus taught, preached and acted in ways which made it likely that people would see him in this light. For instance, Sanders considers that Jesus deliberately rode a donkey into Jerusalem in order to be seen as fulfilling Zechariah 9:9. Sanders thinks that the main reason for Jesus' crucifixion may well have been Jesus' action in overturning the money changers' tables in the Temple: such an act could have been regarded as sacrilege.

Sanders also says that the gospels include no clear view of the coming kingdom of God. The most that can be said is that it involves a reorientation of values, but these are not clearly defined. The gospels give a variety of different pictures of this kingdom – some are to be looked forward to after death, others are found solely within this world. Sanders suggests that the gospels may faithfully present the diversity of images with which Jesus worked and refuses to adopt any one view as being the 'right' one.

Sanders' approach can be seen as a straightforward rejection of Bultmann's. Thus arguably two of the best-known New Testament scholars of the twentieth century, who strongly influenced scholarship in the times in which they lived, totally disagree with each other.

Others who wish to reject Bultmann's scepticism maintain that most of the material about Jesus was passed on by word of mouth and, therefore, there is a high level of consistency in its content. The gap between the life of Jesus and the first of the written records may be less than thirty-five years. This reinforces the view that details of Jesus' life may have been reasonably accurately transmitted as many people would have known him who were still alive. Within a few years of his death, stories about Jesus were being spread around a wide area, and by 49 AD (roughly sixteen years after the crucifixion) the Acts of the Apostles records a significant meeting at Jerusalem attended by James, Peter, Paul and others who knew Jesus to discuss the future (cf. p. 19). With so many witnesses to Jesus' life and such a short period of time having elapsed, the scope for manifest distortions in the story of Jesus can be argued to be much smaller than many scholars allow.

This by no means solves the problem, however, as there is no way of knowing which of Jesus' sayings are accurate and which are later additions. In the first three gospels Jesus speaks only in short sentences, often drawing on nature as his source. Even where these sayings have been combined, as in the Sermon on the Mount (Matthew 5:3ff), it is possible to detect the smaller units which have been put together to create the final effect. Only in Mark 13 and its parallels in Matthew and Luke is there a long speech by Jesus. By contrast, in John's gospel Jesus is portrayed as making long and complicated speeches which drew on Jewish traditions and festivals. Two different figures are thus presented – which is the true Jesus?

N. Perrin (*Rediscovering the Teachings of Jesus*, p. 39) argues that in order to arrive at the authentic sayings of Jesus the burden of proof must lie with those who wish to claim authenticity. It is not, in other words, up to the critic of historicity to establish a position, it is up to the advocates of historicity to maintain their claim in the face of a presumption that most of the gospel material is not historical. Scholars who come to the gospels from the study of Greek and Roman history tend to be far less sceptical about the historicity of much of the biblical material than many New Testament scholars. They would find Perrin's approach difficult to understand.

The evidence is conflicting and there are no simple answers, but that does not mean that some answers may not be possible, as Sanders indicates. At times the issues will be complex but there may be no alternative to complexity. At the least, it may be possible to attain a greater degree of understanding about the gospels than was possible even twenty years ago and to see that simple answers may distort the truth.

In this chapter we have looked at various attempts to locate Jesus in his time and to interpret him from an assumed perspective. In the final section of this book we will return to examine the issue of the truth of the gospel stories in more detail.

NINE

The Four and Forty Gospels

Alternative texts

The gospels are 'lives of Jesus' written by four evangelists using the sources, both oral and written, available to them. However there are other gospels, called the apocryphal gospels, which consist of a wide range of material. Some of these are fragmentary and deal with particular aspects of Jesus' life. This material can be grouped under headings based on the subjects they deal with: infancy gospels, gospels dealing with Jesus' teaching, passion gospels, and resurrection gospels. The following is a basic list of the more important material in three of the categories:

Infancy Texts
• the book of James
• the gospel of Thomas
• the gospel of Pseudo-Matthew
• the gospel of the birth of Mary
• the Arabic gospel of the infancy
• the history of Joseph the carpenter
• four versions of the Coptic lives of the Virgin

Passion and Resurrection Texts
• the gospel of Peter
• the acts of Pilate or the gospel of Nicodemus
• thirteen fragments of Coptic narratives of the ministry and Passion
• the gospel of Bartholomew

- the gospel according to the Hebrews
- the book of the resurrection of Christ by Bartholomew
- the book of John the evangelist
- the assumption of the Virgin (which exists in twelve versions, including Coptic, Greek, Latin and Syriac)

There are five more fragments from what are called the Nag Hammadi texts, some of which concentrate on the teaching by Jesus to his disciples. These include the gospel of Truth and the gospel according to the Egyptians. The Nag Hammadi texts (discovered in the 1940s) are a collection of works containing ideas not generally found in the canonical Christian books. These texts were based on Gnostic ideas, essentially revolving around the passing on of secret knowledge which would aid initiates in attaining the union of their soul, the 'divine spark', with God.

The apocryphal gospels were all trying to convey particular messages about Jesus. Therefore it is necessary, in examining them, to try to work out what they were trying to do. An examination of these gospels can help the reader to see more clearly the theological slant of the four biblical gospels.

Infancy narratives

Only two of the four gospels which were included in the canon, Matthew and Luke, contain details of Jesus' birth. Both of these accounts concentrate on other characters in the story, and light is thrown on Jesus through the actions of these others. Matthew's aim was to show that Jesus was the true Messiah expected by the Jews and his gospel has, therefore, lists of descendants to show Jesus' legitimacy as being descended from King David. Luke's account, on the other hand, shows Jesus fulfilling the hopes of the OT yet also reaching out beyond the confines of the Jewish boundaries.

In the infancy gospel of Thomas (not the same as the better known gospel of Thomas, which is a collection of Jesus' sayings) the text begins with the child Jesus – there is no birth story. The stories concentrate on the wonders that the boy performs. For instance,

Jesus is portrayed as making sparrows of mud which then come alive and fly away; bringing to life a playmate who had had an accident; healing a boy's foot; and helping his carpenter father, Joseph, by lengthening a beam which he had cut too short. These latter incidents are all positive – they are 'wonders' held to be performed by Jesus. However the text also includes scenes in which Jesus curses other children. The aim of this material is clearly to demonstrate Jesus' power.

These stories are not considered to be historical accounts. They are rather intended to show that Jesus, even when he was a child, was already someone special, having powers that went beyond those of any normal human boy. The aim is to show Jesus' true nature as having a divine origin, or at least Jesus being empowered by God from his earliest years. Even the cursing stories have a role in reminding the reader of the need to be cautious when in the presence of a person of power, even if he appears to be merely a boy.

A greater awareness of the theological interests in infancy stories can help modern readers to see more clearly the theology within the gospels. For instance, in Matthew and Luke's gospels there are stories of Jesus' childhood and the question immediately arises as to whether these should be given the same historical status as the stories in the gospel of Thomas. Jesus in these stories is only portrayed as a baby but nevertheless he is shown as a divinely conceived baby and his mother is held to be a virgin. This story could be viewed as being even more miraculous than the stories in Thomas' gospels. In fact, the virgin birth story may be the basis for the later stories in that it is because he is conceived without human agency that he has the powers attributed to him. These powers are hidden: Jesus looks like an ordinary baby and grows into an apparently ordinary child and then a man. His divine origin has to be recognized and is not obvious. The stories in Luke and Matthew cannot, therefore, be regarded as essentially different in kind from those in Thomas and reasons need to be given why the reader should accept one set of accounts as being historically accurate and not the other. Or, to put it the other way round, why one should not dismiss both Luke and Matthew's account if one has already rejected that of Thomas.

Passion narratives

The Acts of Pilate (also called the gospel of Nicodemus) is one of the better examples of an apocryphal Passion gospel. The Acts of Pilate begins with the arrest of Jesus by the Jewish authorities and the same basic story is told as in the four canonical gospels, however there are more scenes in this text. The point of the additions is to help the reader to see more clearly the wrong that was being done in condemning Jesus to death. The extra material aims to show both:

a) the error of those who recognized Jesus as of special significance and yet who refused to stand up for him, and
b) that the Jewish authorities refused to see who he was. This is portrayed as a deliberate act of will by the Jews who were determined to kill him.

These extra stories are entirely consistent with the material in the four gospels and the reader is left convinced that Jesus goes to his death as a result of injustice and that this was due to the hostility of the Jewish leaders. This attitude was to have profound consequences in later centuries when Christian persecution of the Jews reached dreadful proportions. (Dan Cohn-Sherbok's book *The Crucified Jew* (1992) portrays the viciousness and extent of this cruelty practised by Christians and the Christian Church over the centuries.)

Once again, reading apocryphal material helps the modern reader to understand that the biblical stories of Jesus already contain particular attitudes which the authors use to interpret the figure of Jesus. Yet, in the end, when a tiny collection of valued books came to be made, the apocryphal material was omitted. The four gospel books included in the New Testament library contain, by contrast with apocryphal material, the less-heavily theological working out of Jesus' story. However reading the apocryphal gospels encourages the twentieth-century reader to move away from viewing Matthew, Mark, Luke and John as historical biography and instead to see these books as portraying a more theological understanding of Jesus' life.

A question of priority

Did the four gospels in the canon come first and were the apocryphal gospels written as later embellishments, or was the issue more confused? By the second century it is clear that both sets of material existed. For instance, Justin Martyr refers to books which are probably much the same as the Synoptic gospels while Ireneus of Lyons refers to what appear to be the apocryphal gospels. There are no earlier manuscripts so there can be no conclusive evidence as to which texts came first. The gospel of Thomas from the Nag Hammadi texts appears close to the Synoptic tradition and may be about the same date, but most of the apocryphal material is probably a later development – although there is no unanimity on this and some writers have argued for an earlier date.

One motive for holding that the apocryphal gospels are later than Matthew, Mark, Luke and John is that the closer the dates of the two sets of documents, the greater the risk that scepticism about the accuracy of the apocryphal stories may extend to the four gospels. This may, however, be to miss the point. It can be argued that there is very little basis for claiming that the gospels in the canon are historical whilst the apocryphal material is not. Both sets of stories tell about the wonders of Jesus. The early Christians who were historically much closer to the events described may have had reasons for including one set of records rather than another. It is plausible to contend that they may have included Matthew, Mark, Luke and John due to the high regard in which they were held and this may have partly been based on whether they were considered to be trying to remain close to historical truth.

Growth towards recognition

The four gospels were accepted by the early Church well before the acceptance of the full NT canon, which includes all the epistles and other books included in the NT today. This full canon was only accepted in the fourth/fifth century. At the end of the second century Luke's gospel had not been firmly recognized, and as late as 220 AD John's gospel was still meeting considerable opposition. The earliest manuscripts available which have the four gospels together (the Chester Beatty papyri and the Sinaitic Syriac text) are dated about 250 AD, although the heretical gospel of Peter (about 150 AD) seems to show an awareness of these gospels.

Marcion (*c.* 160 AD) founded a Christian community which based itself on a rejection of the Old Testament and a limited acceptance of the gospels and Paul's letters. When other Christian communities condemned this Marcionite church, they argued that it was important to base Christian systems on the right selection of scriptural works. Tatian (also second century AD) tried to harmonize the gospel material into one, single book, rather than accepting a number of parallel accounts. Once again the whole Church could not agree to this and what emerged was four separate accounts. This may have been because particular sections of the Church had each come to identify closely with a single gospel and did not want to see this abandoned; or because these four gospels were the only comprehensive accounts of Jesus' life that were available; or, indeed, that great authority was given to the 'words of the Lord' (of central importance for Paul, for instance) which were found most frequently in the four gospels.

It must be recognized that in the first centuries after Jesus' death there were tremendous disputes between and within Christian communities as to what beliefs were to be held as correct. There were many 'movements' which were eventually considered to be heretical and there was little unanimity in various key areas. Disputes over the gospel texts were similarly fierce and the four gospels as we have them today only emerged as the 'accepted' versions over a period of about 200 or more years. By the fourth century, for instance, the Shepherd of Hermas was still included in the canon and the inclusion of the Epistle to the Hebrews was much debated.

It therefore took considerable time, and many disputes, before the 'fixed book list' represented by the canon of the NT available today finally emerged. However this does not solve all the problems raised in Chapter 1, rather it opens up wider horizons for gospel research and it is to these we now turn.

TEN

Dissecting the Evidence

Imagine someone has been murdered. An autopsy has to be performed on the body and the doctors have to determine how s/he came to die. Each piece of evidence is sifted and examined with care. There are some parallels here to the study of the gospels. The 'body' is the four gospels we have available to us today; the task is to understand how they came to be written. In order to complete the task, the evidence will have to be carefully examined for clues.

There are two initial problems. First, one needs to arrive at the original text of the four gospels. This involves examination of the manuscripts. Second, one needs to examine the origins of the four gospels themselves. This involves scholars trying to 'go behind' the manuscripts to see how they developed.

The manuscripts

The first task has been made slightly easier by the discovery of a number of manuscripts dating from the early centuries of the Church, the most important of which are:

a) in 1859 a Greek Bible copied in the fourth century was found at St Catherine's monastery in Sinai. This is the *Codex Sinaiticus* and is in the British Museum. This contained the twenty-seven books of the NT as well as the Epistle of Barnabas and the Shepherd of Hermas.

b) the *Codex Vaticanus*, which had been held in the Vatican since about 1450, was revealed widely for the first time in the mid-nineteenth century and again dates from the mid-fourth century.

c) in 1562 Theodore Beza recovered from the monastery of St Ireneus in Lyons a fifth-century Latin/Greek copy of the gospels and Acts. This is now held at Cambridge University, England.

d) in 1627 the Greek text of the *Codex Alexandrinus* was presented as a gift to King Charles I from the Patriarch of Constantinople. Its dating was similar to c) but received more attention by scholars.

e) in 1930 Chester Beatty acquired three mid-third century papyri which included the gospels and Acts.

f) in 1955 Martin Bodmer acquired what has been called the *Bodmer papyrus* containing the gospel of John written about 200 AD. This is the earliest source of one of the gospels.

All the above texts are considered to have come originally from the Egyptian Christian Church, and a) and b) represent the most reliable versions available to scholars. It may well have been that different forms of the gospels were available in different places and this may have been one reason for the reluctance of the early Church Fathers to accept a single gospel.

In general, there are few manuscripts available dated earlier than the fifth century AD, in other words a gap of more than 400 years after the events they recorded took place. This is a considerable timespan and poses a problem for scholars, although writings of the early Church Fathers, of which many have survived, can help to verify the text of the gospels in places. With the growth in the Christian Church, once the gospels had been consigned to parchment and were more widely available, the scope for alterations may have been lessened. The early Fathers would have been at pains to bring together the texts which commanded the broadest agreement. Even today, however, there is still the possibility of the discovery of earlier manuscripts which may throw light on the texts.

Texts in Greek

Although Jesus and his followers probably spoke Aramaic all the above manuscripts are written in Greek, which was a common language for educated people across the Roman world. From these and other manuscripts the International New Testament Project (founded in 1948) has produced a core version of each gospel by comparing and contrasting the textual variations found across all known texts. It must be recognized, however, that the material they are working with is dated well after the events the gospels describe.

Texts in Latin

The confusion among the early Latin manuscripts led the then Pope Damasus to request Jerome to make an authoritative version of the NT. Jerome made a careful comparison of the earliest Greek manuscripts and only made a change in the by then accepted Latin phrasing when it was essential to reflect the original meaning. Jerome's version, completed in 383 AD and known as the Vulgate, has had an enormous influence and most later translations were made from it. Jerome's efforts were, however, criticized at the time and many of his contemporaries refused to use his version, although it was eventually generally accepted.

Texts in other languages

Apart from the Vulgate, Coptic and Arabic versions are all later than the manuscripts referred to above. The Syriac versions are notably important, particularly assuming the first records of Jesus' teaching would have been in Aramaic (which is similar to Syriac). The Aramaic would have been translated into Greek and then into Syriac. These texts are also relatively early (from about the fifth century AD).

Problems with the text

Modern versions of the Bible attempt to be as faithful as possible to the earliest texts available, although the influence of editors and translators can be clear when comparing even texts in English. A clear example is the passage from 1 John 5:7–8, where the New Revised Standard Version has:

> There are three that testify: the Spirit and the water and the blood, and these three agree.

This is radically different from the old King James Version of the Bible which renders the same line as follows:

> For there are three that bear record in heaven, the Father, the Word and the Holy Ghost: and these three are one. And there are three that bear witness in earth, the Spirit, and the water, and the blood: and these three agree in one.

There is conflicting evidence in the original texts. The King James Version follows the most extensive variant of the text, which is known to have been composed in the fourth/fifth centuries to amplify the text in the Latin version and was unknown in the Greek version. It only won gradual acceptance. The NRSV, by contrast, is based on the version that is considered to have been original.

It should also be recognized that in Greek uncial texts there is no punctuation and this can lead to significant variations between texts. It can be worth looking at the ending of Mark's gospel and John 1:3–4 to see how different the translation may be if punctuation is inserted in different places, as it is in some modern translations.

The oral gospel tradition

The second and central problem when studying the gospels is the gap between the life and death of Jesus and the written accounts that are now available. In this period, stories about Jesus were handed down by word of mouth and in writing. However the tradition concerning Jesus was not set in stone. As people reflected on his life, development would have taken place. There are, therefore, four levels involved in the production of one of the gospels:

• Jesus' life and death;
• the views of the early Christian community which preserved the stories about Jesus;
• the way in which the evangelist shaped the material;
• subsequent variations in the text.

The first three levels are reflected in the main approaches followed in the study of the gospels since the nineteenth century. **Source criticism** looks for the earlier documents used by the evangelists to compile their accounts; **form criticism** examines the stories of Jesus' teaching which were circulating within the Christian community and how these were brought together; and **redaction criticism** looks at the role of the evangelist as editor or 'redactor' in writing and 'creating' the text. It should be noted that the word 'criticism' here does *not* have its conventional meaning in modern English. It comes from the German and involves analytic study or, to return to the Sherlock Holmes imagery, putting the text under a magnifying glass.

These three methods, which have formed the backbone to the study of the gospels in this century, need to be examined in more detail. They represent the 'dissecting tools' which analysts can use to try to get as close as possible to the evidence.

Source criticism

The aim of source criticism is to uncover earlier stages in the development of texts within the gospels. This approach rests on the theory that there existed shorter written pieces of work which were brought together by the different gospel writers. If, then, it is possible to work back to arrive at these original sources one can come closer to the original accounts of Jesus and these can then be more effectively assessed. (To introduce some technical language, the search for earlier texts is often described as seeking for the Proto-work or the *Ur* text or the *Vorlage*. There is no need to be confused by these terms, however, as they all refer to the prior documents which underlie the present books.)

A 'shorthand' way of describing source criticism is to look on it as a 'scissors and paste' exercise. In other words, the attempt is made to identify the pieces that have been 'stuck together' to form the gospel we now have available to us. Identifying the individual pieces is intended to bring scholars closer to the original texts of the gospels. The source critic assumes that coherent narratives have been woven together to form the existing texts and the aim is to recover the original narratives.

An example may illustrate the procedure. If one looks at Matthew's gospel, a great deal of the text is also found in Mark. If Mark comes before Matthew (see Chapter 11), then Matthew has used Mark as a source and has shaped this material for his own purposes. There is other material in Matthew which is shared with Luke but is not found in Mark. This material seems to be a collection of Jesus' sayings and it can be argued, therefore, that this is a second major source for Matthew's ideas. There are no existing copies of this text in its original form so it has been called simply 'a source' and is described as 'Q' (from the German *Quelle*). Most of Matthew's gospel, therefore, can be accounted for by two sources – Mark and 'Q'.

In this context the term 'source' refers to a written source which can be deduced as underlying an existing gospel. However, the word is sometimes used more generally to describe short snatches of material incorporated in the four gospels. These would not have been whole texts in themselves but more isolated extracts, perhaps passed down orally. One line of recent scholarship on 'Q' has come to see this not as a single source but rather a set of shorter material all of which may not have been used by Matthew and Luke.

The pioneer of New Testament source criticism was J.J. Griesbach (1745–1812) who recognized the differences between John and the other three gospels. He saw that Matthew, Mark and

Luke have much in common and that the four books could not be harmonized into a single account. More recently, B.H. Streeter (1874–1937) wrote *The Four Gospels: A Study of Origins* which became the classic treatment of the sources of the Synoptic gospels even though some of the ideas were disputed. (The sources of the Synoptic gospels are dealt with in more detail in Chapter 11.)

Form criticism

Whereas source criticism looks for the short texts which have been incorporated into the present gospel books, form criticism seeks to identify each individual unit which makes up the text – the building blocks from which the writer assembled his account. If source criticism might be termed a 'scissors and paste' exercise, then form criticism might be described as a 'jigsaw' approach. The aim of form criticism is to identify the individual, small jigsaw pieces which, it is held, were assembled together to form the gospel now available to us. In many cases these pieces may be very small – as little as half a verse – although they may also be somewhat larger. Form critics assume our existing texts are woven together from small individual scenes and sayings about Jesus and the aim is to recover these.

The earliest stories about Jesus were, without doubt, oral. The accounts of what Jesus said and did were passed on in a short form – just the 'bare bones' of the stories were memorized and retold. However, as the preacher or teacher in the early Church communities used these stories, he or she may have added more detail and made the story more interesting and easier to understand in terms of its ultimate relevance to questions of religious faith. It was this expanded material which the evangelists used to produce their 'biographies' of Jesus.

Form critics presume that it is logically possible to trace, within the gospels, the short original accounts of what Jesus said and to find the actual words and actions of the historical Jesus. However, in practice, it is not easy to carry out this dissection of the texts. We have only the expanded versions of the Jesus story with which to work, and there is no guaranteed set of scholarly tools which will enable the original material to be ascertained. As an example, the shorter version of the story *may* be the original which has subsequently been expanded, but it could also be a later summary of the original passage.

Form critics have identified two main categories of literary building blocks in the gospels: sayings of Jesus and stories about Jesus.

Sayings of Jesus

Modern scholarship has highlighted three types of sayings. The first is where there is usually a short scene-setting passage and then the quotation from Jesus. The saying may be an answer to a question by a disciple or a scribe (for instance, Mark 2:1–12; 2:23–8; 3:1–6; etc.). The second type is the 'logia' of Jesus, where there is no scene-setting, and these contain some religious or general truth. These general religious or moral statements have aroused questions as to their accuracy as similar expressions are found in Jewish Wisdom literature. They may, therefore, have been put on Jesus' lips by the evangelists. An example would be Matthew 12:35:

> The good person brings good things out of a good treasure and the evil person brings evil things out of an evil treasure.

Of course, this could have been said by Jesus, but it is the type of saying common in Jewish rabbinical literature and may well have been attributed to Jesus by the evangelist. The third type of sayings are those about the Law. For instance in Matthew 5:21–2:

> You have heard that it was said to those of ancient times, 'You shall not murder; and whoever murders shall be liable to judgement.' But I say to you that if you are angry with a brother or sister you will be liable to judgement.

These sayings relate to the Jewish Law and Jesus' approach to it. Again, it is difficult to be sure which are authentic sayings of Jesus and which were attributed to him to make a particular point that he (or the evangelist) was concerned about.

Stories about Jesus

The gospels also contain examples of narrative stories about Jesus. The miracle stories (which are dealt with later in a separate chapter) are the clearest example of this type of literature, although there are other examples as well (for instance, Jesus as a child in the Temple or the baptism of Jesus).

In the miracle stories, the position of the sick person is given first and perhaps the ineffectiveness of the doctors is emphasized. Then Jesus' healing action follows and the effectiveness of this action is made clear, as well as the wonder of those who saw it. Jesus' *Word* is portrayed as decisive (see pp. 60–3 and p. 153). The intention of these stories is to bring glory to Jesus.

They may well go back to historical events, but merely because there is a standard literary form being used in no way invalidates, nor validates, the story. The question of authenticity is still open. It may be that the underlying stories express something very like what actually occurred and it has simply been placed into a standard literary framework by the evangelist.

An example might illustrate the problem. In many cases the people with whom Jesus was talking are not identified and it is common to find reference simply to 'scribes and Pharisees'. This is because the identity of these individuals is not important to the point of the story. The aim of the story may be to make a point about what Jesus was saying, and the contributions of others would only be relevant in so far as they help to do this. What is more, at each stage in the development process further details were added by the writers. So the stories about Jesus offer many possible avenues to explore when one is focusing on the 'jigsaw' pieces of a particular account.

Critical criteria for selecting 'original' material

Some scholars have attempted to give criteria which would aid a selection of those parables, sayings or actions which are 'historical' and those which are not. The following are some of the most widely used of such criteria, although there are others.

The criterion of dissimilarity. A saying of Jesus' is more likely to be authentic if it is dissimilar from the teachings of Judaism or the early Church. J. Jeremias (*New Testament Theology 1*, pp. 3–37) takes the opposing view, maintaining that we are justified in assuming authenticity unless inauthenticity can be established. This is a good example of the difficulty of applying these criteria!

The criterion of unintentionality. This criterion looks for those sayings or actions which do not seem to serve the expected intention of the early Christian communities or run counter to it. C.F.D. Moule has assembled a number of pieces of evidence like this. As an example, Moule argues that the idea of Jesus mixing freely with women would have been alien to expectations and to a developing male-dominated community. As he says:

> . . . through all the gospel traditions . . . there comes a remarkably firmly drawn portrait of an attractive young man moving freely about among women of all sorts, including the decidedly disreputable, without a trace of sentimentality, unnaturalness or prudery, and yet, at every point, maintaining a simple integrity of character. (*The Phenomenon of the New Testament*, p. 63)

On this basis, Jesus' reactions to women would be regarded as probably authentic.

The criterion of originality. If a saying of Jesus' appeared to have nothing in common with what might have been expected of a Jewish teacher of the period, it might be more likely to be original and thus to have been authentic. If, for instance, Jesus portrays leaving behind family and other close ties in order to serve God alone, this could be regarded as an original approach to serving God and therefore be authentic.

The criterion of multiple or multiform attestation. A saying recorded in more than one gospel is more likely to be authentic. As an example, the saying about saving and losing one's life appears in Matthew 16:25; Mark 8:35; Luke 9:24 and 17:33; and John 12:25. This saying appears to originate in three sources – Mark, 'Q' and a source used by John. What is more, the difference in wording makes it likely that there were several sources. In this case the saying is said to be supported by 'multiple attestation'. C.H. Dodd (*History and the Gospel*, pp. 86–103) suggested modifying this criterion so that we speak not of multiple *sources* but of multiple *forms*. Thus Jesus' friendship with sinners appears in various forms and is, therefore, likely to be valid.

The Aramaic criterion. Assuming that Jesus spoke Aramaic, there would have been an Aramaic substratum of tradition. If, therefore, any of his sayings could readily be translated into Aramaic, this could increase the likelihood that these were attributable to him rather than having been written by the editors of the gospels.

Each of these criteria has to be considered separately and each carries a certain amount of weight, although no one factor should be regarded as decisive. When taken together, these criteria could be argued to build up to a cumulative or 'probability' case which increases the chances of historical accuracy. The problem with probability approaches such as this is that assessment of probability is highly subjective. Much will depend on individual interpretation of the balance of probability in each case and there is likely to be substantial disagreement.

* * *

The term 'form criticism' was first used by the German theologian Overbeck in 1882. The technique was, however, principally developed by Herman Gunkel who applied it to the OT. It was then adopted by NT scholars. One of the most important early contributions was made by K.L. Schmidt, who showed that each evangelist grouped material together and added details of time and place to provide a historical framework for the story. M. Dibelius was another major form critic. His book *From Tradition to Gospel* (1919) suggested that the gospels had to be seen within the missionary life of the early Christian communities. They are not biographies in the normal sense but rather books which reflect the theological views of those communities. The evangelists were not true authors but rather compilers of material. Bultmann was, perhaps, the most famous of the form critics and his approach has been dealt with on pp. 97–8, 124–5, 146.

Form criticism is invaluable in uncovering the strands and literary types which make up the gospel narratives. If it is used as a way of arriving at the intentions of the different evangelists or the 'setting in life' in which stories arose, it can be very useful (for instance, the setting of the parable of the sheep and the goats is very different in Luke from that in Matthew). However it is illegitimate to move beyond this and to claim that merely because there are different types of stories, possibly later additions to basic stories, or that stories were placed by an editor in a different setting this means that the stories have no historical basis.

Redaction criticism

The result of both the previous methods of research is to leave readers with a series of pieces spread out before them. These methods imply that it is more important to concentrate on the original fragments than the book as a whole. However the gospels are whole books, they are unities. Later scholars have taken this unity seriously and have attempted to work out how each author has adapted his material to his own understanding of Jesus. Thus, If source criticism is described as a 'scissors and paste' approach and form criticism as a 'jigsaw' approach, then redaction criticism involves looking at the picture on the front of the jigsaw box. In other words, looking at the gospels as they are presented to us today rather than seeking the component parts. Redaction critics understand the texts as largely coming from the mind of an editor who 'created' the narrative.

This method of research is not independent of the previous methods since in order to arrive at the final focus of a text it is helpful to know the individual parts which the editor had available for assembly. The argument is that when earlier material has been identified and eliminated one can decide which material was inserted by the editor. Thus Mark 1:1 is composed by the evangelist as an introduction to the book:

The beginning of the good news of Jesus Christ, the Son of God.

Similarly Mark 1:9 is thought to be the work of the editor:

In those days Jesus came from Nazareth of Galilee and was baptized by John in the Jordan.

Sometimes this editorial work, which is necessary to make the gospel a unity, is longer, for instance Mark 1:14–15, which is also attributed to the editor.

As well as putting in connecting passages of text, the editor shaped existing material to fit his overall view of Jesus. As set out above, the major source for Matthew and Luke (apart from Mark) is considered to be a collection of sayings ('Q'). The editor of Matthew has chosen to put these sayings in a block as the Sermon on the Mount, whereas the editor of Luke has situated the same material at a different place and time in the story. This 'shaping' of the story would be the main purpose of an editor: to bring together as a unity what had previously been disconnected pieces of tradition. By studying the work of the editor one can come to appreciate his understanding of Jesus and how he used the material available to convey this understanding.

There have been major studies in this field and four examples can be summarized as follows:

1   W. Wrede in *The Messianic Secret* (1901, translated into English in 1971) claims that the editor of Mark gives the gospel an overall shape based on the theme of Jesus' commands to his disciples to be silent. Whenever Jesus performs a wonder in Mark he tells the person who is helped not to tell others the name of his helper. The secrecy theme prepares the reader for an unexpected theme: a crucified rather than an obviously victorious Messiah. The crucifixion *is* victory, but only to those who acknowledge Jesus as the Messiah and who understand that his apparent failure to control events is temporary.

2   Rudolf Bultmann in *The Gospel of John* (1941, translated into English in 1971) argues that the fourth gospel focuses on the identity of Jesus as one who comes as a stranger from heaven to impart essential truths about God and salvation. He maintains that Jesus is portrayed as a cosmic redeemer figure coming into this world to show the truth about how life should be lived. This approach is similar to the religious beliefs of a first-century group called the Mandeans (whose writings are still preserved). It is also in line with the views of Gnostic groups in the first and second centuries who argued that salvation consists of knowledge of the truth and that truth could only be arrived at through encountering a heavenly messenger who teaches secret knowledge to chosen human beings. Bultmann holds that John sees Jesus as uniquely occupying this role as heavenly revealer.

Bultmann was over-impressed by images also found in Mandean texts which were developed within an isolated group of early Jewish Christians. The Mandean texts are dated centuries later than the gospels and no other text has been found to support Bultmann's 'cosmic redeemer' theory. Our knowledge of Gnostic texts has also increased very substantially since he wrote his book and, again, these texts do not support his conclusions.

3   J. Kingsbury in his book *Matthew* (1971) has argued that the evangelist has imposed a two-part structure on his material. Part One deals with salvation in the time of Israel (effectively from creation to the time of Jesus' parents), and Part Two with salvation through Jesus the Messiah. This structure allows Jesus to be seen as the fulfilment of Old Testament traditions. (Examples of this have been given in the chapters on the individual gospels.)

4   H. Conzelmann in *The Theology of St Luke* (1960) has argued that the writer of Luke/Acts situates Jesus within a broad time framework. At the beginning, Luke 1 portrays the old Israel based on the piety of Elizabeth and Zechariah. This sets the scene for the time of Jesus, which is inaugurated through Mary being willing to accept her pregnancy as due to God. The rest of Luke unfolds the story of the mission and teaching of Jesus. The time of Jesus then gives way to the period of the formation of Christian communities, and within these communities the message of salvation is proclaimed in the name of Jesus. This is dealt with in the Acts of the Apostles. All of this material, brought together, forms the story of salvation offered to human beings.

None of the above theories about the overall message of the gospels is agreed upon by all scholars. However all of them were, in their time, trend-setting studies in redaction criticism.

Assessment of critical methods

The above represents a brief outline of the main methods of biblical criticism and their advantages. However there are problems with all the above methods and these need to be recognized.

In the case of source criticism, there are no copies of the original texts so one is firmly in the realm of speculation. Much depends on the perception of twentieth-century scholars of how a first-century disciple might have worked. No certainty at all is possible. Much the same can be said of form criticism. The only documents we have are complete works and although rules can be invented to try to move behind these works (for instance, that shorter and less developed stories are likely to be earlier), these really rest on not much more than speculation. A shorter and simpler version could, as we have seen, be a later summary of a more developed earlier tradition. There is a danger in creating structures from a twentieth-century perspective which can then be used to push the text into a form which is acceptable to us.

If it is not feasible to get back to the original material with any surety, then it is also not possible to be certain what an editor has added. It is possible that the community in which the editor worked and any background influences severely limited the editor's freedom to alter what had been handed down. It is also possible that he had a much more free hand. Then again, it is possible that the evangelists had first or at least second-hand knowledge of Jesus which they added to the other material. Mark 1:23–6 can be taken as an example. This deals with the healing of a man with an unclean spirit. It seems almost impossible to determine which parts represent a previous tradition and which are due to the work of the editor. Did Jesus actually say and do everything recorded in these verses, or was there simply a story that he healed someone and the dialogue was then added? Did the dialogue come from a written or oral tradition, or was it wholly or partly the work of the editor? No certainty can be achieved.

In the end, all that one can say with absolute certainty is that perhaps the most remarkable aspect of the text of the gospels is the excellence of its transmission over nearly 2,000 years.

Reader and text criticism

Any written material is composed to communicate with a reader, and certainly this is the case with the gospels. In the writer's mind is a dialogue which will go on between the reader and the book. The writer, if he or she is a good writer, encourages this dialogue by the style of writing used. The 'reader and text' or 'reader–response' method arose from the difficulties with the previously outlined methods. It was held that it does not matter *where* the text came from or *how* it came to be written but what *we*, the individual reader, can find in the text.

J.D. Crossan in *Parables: The Challenge of the Historical Jesus* (1973) helpfully explains how the reader and the text are related in the case of the parables. He suggests that the nature of parable writing is that it is open-ended. In other words, this style assumes the involvement of the reader and is intended to provoke a particular response. Clearly Jesus wanted to provoke a response from those to whom he spoke; similarly the evangelist (the editor) wants to provoke a response. The aim is not to leave the reader uninterested – the text is meant to have an effect. The purpose is not to get the reader to think 'What would Jesus' audience have thought?', but 'How do I respond to this teaching?' These are very different positions. The first question sees the text as something objective and the reader is essentially irrelevant. In the second question, however, the response of the reader is central. The evangelist's aim, therefore, is to deliberately draw the reader into being a participant in Jesus' life as he reads about it. The intent is to affect the reader and, indeed, to change his or her life.

The use of an anonymous narrator who tells the story helps this style. The narrator holds the story together for the reader, supplying any details which the reader needs to make sense of the text. The narrator is the scene-shifter, interpreter and all-seeing observer who is able to explain what is 'really' going on in the minds of the characters. In Matthew 16, for example, the disciples respond inadequately to what Jesus says and it is the editor/evangelist who explains the real meaning:

Jesus said to them, 'Watch out and beware of the yeast of the Pharisees and Sadducees.' They said to one another, 'It is because we have brought no bread.' And becoming aware of it Jesus said, 'You of little faith, why are you talking about having no bread? Do you still not perceive? . . . How could you fail to perceive that I was not speaking about bread? . . .' *Then they understood that he had not told them to beware of the yeast of bread, but of the teaching of the Pharisees and Sadducees.* (Matthew 16:6–12)

The italicized words were obviously inserted by the evangelist to make clear Jesus' point.

A. Culpepper, in *Anatomy of the Fourth Gospel* (1983), has made a study of John using reader-response criticism. He has shown that it is possible to analyse a gospel as a piece of literature and to arrive at suggested messages which the editor wished the reader to take up. This is a helpful way of proceeding but it is not without its own problems. One is required to read back from the text to the original situation and to try to arrive at the intentions of the author. Given the time lapse and the very different thought-world in which the gospels were written, this is exceptionally difficult. Again, one is into the realm of speculation, and this time speculation about the writer who we think chose to write like this.

Different people will, of course, respond differently to the biblical material. For instance, liberation theologians working with the poor in South America will look to the gospels for messages about justice and freedom from oppression, whereas feminists will look for evidence of male domination and suppression of women, as well as the recovery of the significance of women in the gospels (see Chapter 15).

Conclusion

Much biblical scholarship and the enormous effort that has gone into it may lead nowhere. It may be a case of sincere, dedicated scholars busily working hard to achieve very little, except one more theory which rests largely on conjecture and which will in turn be replaced by a new theory a few years later. Certainly little consensus is emerging from all the effort that has been expended on biblical scholarship to date.

The tools used to dissect the body of the gospel material are of some help, but they all need to be approached with caution. Certainly any one method of research will lead to failure. If, however, a variety of approaches is used and the answers produced by one method are balanced against those of another, then we can get further than simply reading the text with our twentieth-century eyes and assuming that what we understand as the meaning is all that can be found. In other words, one does not have to resort to an uncritical approach simply because there is no single scholarly and critical approach which provides a guaranteed way forward.

ELEVEN

The Synoptic Tradition

The gospels of Matthew, Mark and Luke are very similar in style and content, whereas John has a different tone. Because of this difference in approach, the first three gospels are often considered together as the 'Synoptic tradition'. By and large, all three Synoptic texts treat Jesus in the same way.

The Synoptic problem

The 'Synoptic tradition' is a modern term used to describe the fact that of 661 verses in Mark about 80 per cent are found in Matthew and about 65 per cent in Luke. If one prints the texts side by side in three columns it is easy to see which parts of the books are the same in content even if the editors did not always use the material in the same order. Books are available which produce the gospels in this form (such as *Synoptic Parallels*, edited by H.D. Sparks) and this is a very helpful aid to study.

This raises, however, what W. Farmer has termed 'the Synoptic problem': it is clear that the books are in some way dependent on each other but it is not clear in what way. The key issue is which book came first and how did the other two texts use the existing material? Various solutions have been proposed and they can be grouped into three categories:

a) one of the three gospels came first and the others were developments of that initial work;

b) All three gospels were produced independently but they shared a common core of material from a common source;

c) prior to the present books, there existed other written texts which have now disappeared but on which the present texts depend.

One of the three gospels came first

The first issue is which of the three gospels has priority. Although arguments have been put forward for the priority of Luke, few scholars accept these. The choice rests between the priority of Mark or of Matthew, and these possibilities can be dealt with in turn.

The priority of Mark   This is the view held by most modern scholars: that the shortest text, Mark, was written first. Matthew and Luke copied Mark independently of each other. Before Mark there would have been an oral tradition about Jesus and, possibly, a collection of written materials which grouped together elements in a continuous text. Mark then becomes the source gospel used by both Matthew and Luke independently. This is supported by the fact that both Matthew and Luke follow roughly the same sequence of scenes used in Mark.

This idea works well, but when the Marcan material is taken out of Matthew and Luke's gospels there remains quite a substantial amount of text. Much of this remainder is made up of Jesus' sayings and is similar in both books. To explain this scholars have suggested that a second early text existed, made up of these sayings. This text is named 'Q'. Whereas 'Q' was once considered a single source, now scholars tend to think it may have been a collection of sayings as both Matthew and Luke use the material in a different order.

In a few cases, Matthew and Luke have the same reading of a passage whilst Mark has a different version. This makes it seem as if Matthew and Luke knew each other's texts. An example of this is in Mark 6:31–4 where Jesus takes his disciples to a lonely place. Matthew and Luke both omit 'Many saw them coming and going' (6:33) and 'they were as sheep without a shepherd' (6:34). Examples such as this reduce the plausibility of the idea that Mark was, separately, the source for Luke and Matthew.

Another counter argument to the priority of Mark is that there are instances in which Mark and Luke appear to have copied Matthew. This appears to be the case, for instance, when Jesus is accused of being in league with Satan (Matthew 12:22–37; Mark 3:20–30; Luke 11:14–23). Also in Matthew 22:34–40, where Jesus describes the greatest commandment, parallel versions of this scene indicate that Mark (12:28–34) and Luke (10:25–8) have little contact with each other, whereas Matthew and Mark and Matthew and Luke appear to know each other's texts.

The priority of Matthew   The earliest view to be held was that Matthew had priority, and Church traditions affirmed this. Eusebius' *Church History*, written in the fourth century and quoting a letter from Papias (cf. p. 83), said that:

> Matthew collected the oracles in the Hebrew language and each [Mark and Luke] interpreted them as best he could. (E.H., 3:xxxix:16)

One problem with the above is that the letter from Papias no longer exists and neither does any copy of Matthew written in Hebrew, so verification is not easy.

Griesbach (cf. pp. 116–17), however, took up the idea of the priority of Matthew. He saw Mark as the last of the three Synoptic gospels, providing a short summary of the other two. This idea has some merit in that it explains why Matthew and Luke sometimes differ from Mark. If Luke read Matthew, and Mark knew both books and adapted material from each, this would allow for agreements. The objection to this view is not drawn from technical arguments based on the text but from a more commonsense approach: why would anyone want to write such a summary, particularly one which omits some favourite stories about Jesus such as the Lord's Prayer and the Beatitudes? It seems highly implausible, but this does not mean it is impossible! There is no way of answering this problem since there is no evidence outside the gospels themselves, but it seems an unlikely ordering.

The three gospels were produced independently of each other

This is an ingenious solution which dissolves the Synoptic problem. If the three evangelists wrote independently of each other, then there is no problem to solve. It can be argued that each evangelist, probably working in different parts of the Mediterranean world, drew on a common pool of material about Jesus and produced a separate gospel. Because it was a common pool, they sometimes chose to use the same material in their books. This possibility is reinforced by the likelihood that certain of the traditions were already popular in teaching and worship. As an example, if John the Baptist was such a popular preacher that some people were tempted to make him equal to Jesus, it is likely that different evangelists would each have felt it important to include passages which showed that he was subordinated to Jesus in God's plans (cf. Matthew 3:11; Mark 1:7–8; Luke 3:16; John 1:26–7).

A variant on this approach is to be found in the work of M. Goulder, who has suggested that if one accepts that Matthew and Luke were authors in their own right, many of the textual difficulties can be resolved. He holds that Matthew worked from Mark and the Old Testament. Any material not attributable to these sources Goulder suggests was written by the editor of Matthew. Luke worked from Mark, Matthew and the Old Testament. Once again, any material not attributable to these sources was written by the editor of Luke. This means that Matthew and Luke respectively are not simply editors of other material but authors in their own right. Goulder eliminates 'Q' as a source. Material attributed by other scholars to 'Q' is accounted for by the original contributions of Matthew and Luke respectively.

The main problem with maintaining that the gospels were produced independently of each other is that, although it has considerable appeal, the relationship between the texts in the three gospels is so very close in places that this can only be explained by a theory which allows for some of the writers to have had knowledge of the work of the others. However, the theory of the independent production of the gospels does have considerable advantages and it would be wrong to dismiss it too quickly.

The gospels depend on pre-existent material

If the simple solutions do not work, then it may be necessary to try more complicated ones! There may well have been a series of documents both in Aramaic and in Greek concerning the life of Jesus which formed the basis of the texts now known to us. Our present texts may, therefore, relate to each other not only through the gospels with which people today are familiar, but also through earlier material which has now ceased to exist. These possible earlier texts are termed 'Proto-gospels', '*Ur*' gospels' or '*Vorlage* texts' (*Ur* is German for 'primeval' or 'very ancient' and *Vorlage* means 'underlying source'. German scholarship has traditionally dominated biblical studies, hence the use of their terms.)

This has been one of the growth areas in current potential answers to the Synoptic problem. A high level of argument has now developed postulating a variety of potential sources.

Simple version based on Proto-gospels　A simple solution to the problem posits an earlier and a later version of Mark – both of which were available to Matthew and Luke. Thus:

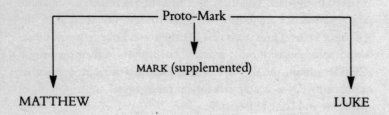

An alternative to this theory is as follows:

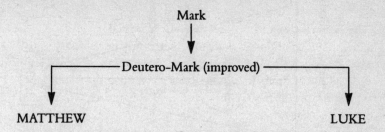

Both these versions are set out in *Studying the Synoptic Gospels* by Sanders and Davies (p. 74). In these plans, 'Mark' indicates the text of Mark which we have in our Bibles today. 'Proto-Mark' indicates an earlier form of this gospel which had less material in it. 'Deutero-Mark' describes a later version of the gospel than the one in the NT. This later text had been expanded by new material which was then available to other evangelists. Both of these variants allow for two versions of Mark having been available to Matthew and Luke. The first version suggests that they knew an earlier and simpler text. The second suggests that Matthew and Luke had access to a later and more developed form of Mark.

Although simple adjustments like these can explain some of the agreements between Matthew and Luke against the version of Mark which we know, they do not make allowances for variations in the text where sometimes Matthew and Luke agree against Mark but where, at other times, it is Matthew and Mark that agree against Luke. To sum up, this means that in most occasions Mark appears to be the earliest gospel, but this is not always the case.

Complex version based on Proto-gospels Set out below are two more complicated variants on the two-source theory. The first is F. C. Grant's theory. The second more complicated variant is M. E. Boismard's theory.

Different Text – Sources by Region/Town

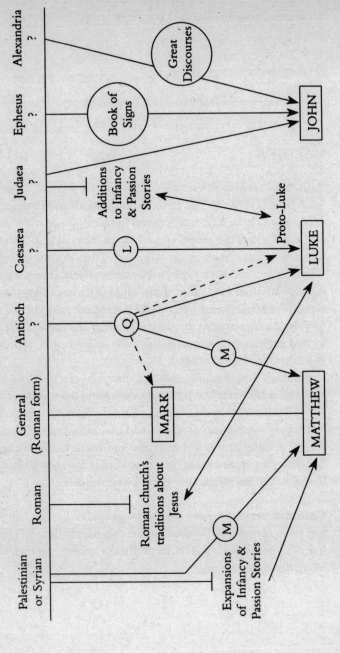

M. E. Boisnard's Theory

| Primitive gospels | | Intermediate gospels which are nearing present form of M/M/L | | Final gospels |

Grant added to the basic theory the view that the evangelists also had access to oral tradition. This degree of complexity is the result of allowing for all the alterations of agreement and disagreement which can be traced between the gospels currently available. It assumes that all the gospel material has a source. Of course, this may not be the case. The evangelist may himself have put in material which he did not obtain from elsewhere.

Boismard's solution also allows for multiple sources. It is based on the view that there existed not only multiple documents but also multiple editions of each document (represented in the diagram by 'Middle Matthew and Mark' and 'Proto-Luke' – where 'Proto' refers to the earliest gospel and 'Middle' to an intermediate development). The final form of each gospel was dependent on the earlier version of at least two of the Synoptic gospels. This theory explains overlaps between Matthew and Luke; the fact that there are signs of the particular style of one evangelist within another Synoptic text; and the way in which Mark and 'Q' overlap.

The main unresolved difficulty is why the present version of Mark came to be written at all since it is held to be a shorter and less fruitful gospel than its forerunner. Boismard suggests that the final version of Mark used the intermediate version of Matthew as well as the intermediate Luke which both included 'Q'.

The two complicated solutions to the Synoptic problem set out above rely on a complex system of multiple sources and, sometimes, multiple editions of Synoptic gospel books. This is the only way forward if one wishes to assert any version of the two-source theory (that Matthew and Luke depend on Mark and 'Q') or any claim that the gospels depend on each other, while at the same time allowing for the subtleties of the connections between passages contained within existing books.

Evaluation

Goulder's approach has great attractions because it cuts through the complexities at one stroke. 'Occam's razor' holds that one should always prefer a simpler theory to a more complex one and on this basis Goulder scores highly. However Goulder's approach does not account for the fact that sometimes Matthew seems to have been used by both Mark and Luke, and Mark may have used Matthew and Luke. Nevertheless, in the absence of any single satisfactory theory, Goulder's approach may have merit.

The modern NT in most Bibles, with its set text and few alternative readings, simply did not exist in the first centuries after Jesus. This makes it difficult to establish what is the core version of a passage and what are its variations. If this cannot be established, then it becomes almost impossible to see how the interweaving lines of textual development can be arrived at, as these are based on the text we have rather than the text the evangelist wrote.

It must also be recognized that the earliest traditions of Jesus may have been passed on in Aramaic, whereas the gospels that we have are in Greek (see pp. 86–7, 111–14). We do not even know, therefore, whether there were originally Aramaic gospels. Or, if there were, how close the original Greek texts may have been to these, still less what development occurred between the texts available to us and the original Greek.

There are no solutions – only many theories. There seems no way of arriving at one understanding of the connections between Matthew, Mark and Luke which may be more probable than any other. What we do have is three separate books which each convey a message. As we have seen, these three texts exist as coherent wholes, with a beginning, a middle and an end.

TWELVE

The Johannine Tradition

In this chapter the 'Johannine tradition' will be examined. This is the name given to the gospel and the two letters of John, taken as a whole. It presents the same essential message about Jesus as the other gospels but it does so in a distinctive way, using material which is not always found elsewhere.

Johannine language

The key word in the Johannine tradition is *love*. God is portrayed as mainly a God of love who wants to establish a relationship of love with human beings. This love is shown from the beginnings of creation, and Jesus, as Son of God, comes to reveal the true nature of God's character. Jesus is prepared to go through great suffering, in the crucifixion, to further God's work. In Jesus, the divine Word, God himself suffers on the cross, and does so out of love. Jesus confirms this when he speaks of his own death as a part of God's purpose (13:31–5).

It is love which holds together Jesus and his followers. As an example, in the Last Supper scenes Jesus commands his disciples to imitate him:

> I give you a new commandment that you love one another; just as I have loved you . . . (13:34)

The central issue for John is that Jesus *reveals* God's purpose to human beings. Jesus *is* the revelation that God loves the world. This results in Jesus being portrayed not as an earthly king but as a heavenly figure who comes to this world from his kingdom which embraces the whole universe. Thus when Pilate questions Jesus, he replies:

> My kingdom is not from this world; . . . For this I was born, and for this I came into the world, to testify to the truth. (18:36–7)

The Johannine tradition has a very limited vocabulary and this is one of its distinctive features. There are endless repetitions of the same words, particularly love, truth, life, light and world. Often words are not used by themselves but in pairs of opposites: light versus dark, or above versus below. Jesus is light from above and he has nothing to do with darkness which is aligned with the world. Following this understanding of Jesus, readers of John must seek light from heaven and keep the dark world at a distance.

In addition, some words which are common in the other gospels are given a special meaning by John, such as 'follow', 'see' and 'remain'. 'Following' usually refers to the task of identifying with Jesus as the revealer of truth, whilst 'seeing' indicates the inner understanding that Jesus is, indeed, God's messenger. 'Abiding' or 'remaining' is a key term in the Last Supper speeches of Jesus, where he describes the need to 'abide in him' in order that God, in turn, can abide in the believer (15:1–11).

Sometimes the words used in John's gospel have both ordinary and special meanings, as in 1:35–51. The first disciples of Jesus are called by their new master and see Jesus at work, follow in his company and stay with him for the day. At a deeper level, however, this gives a model for all disciples to live by: they need to 'see', 'follow' and 'stay with' Jesus. It is the task of every disciple to ask where God can be found, to seek the truth about the world and the presence of God within it, and then to remain faithful to that truth. 'Seeing' is not simply a superficial image, rather it reflects the call to a deeper understanding. This is an essential part of John's gospel and it emerges again, for instance, in the story of the man born blind. There is a dramatic irony present, where true blindness has to do with a blindness to God's presence in the world.

Jesus in the Johannine tradition

Jesus is the focus of John's gospel and it is the attitude of people to Jesus that determines where they stand. As an example, Jesus is described as 'the light of the world' (8:12) and those who refuse to believe this are in darkness because they are standing outside God's presence.

The Johannine writings are not simple, face-value texts – they are deeply theological reflections. Jesus is portrayed less as the carpenter's son than as the stranger from heaven. Sometimes this leads readers to separate the Synoptic gospels from John and to see them as historical biography whilst John provides theology. This, however, is an over-simplification which distorts the real position. All four gospels are theological works because the story of Jesus has been moulded in accordance with each author's own views. In this sense, there is no real difference between the four gospels. However it must be accepted that the theology of John's account stands out clearly from the other three and provides a coherent and distinctive viewpoint.

The Johannine perspective is probably the result of several decades of reflection on the part of a Christian community. The effect of this process has been to stress the inner meaning of the life of Jesus rather than the historical events of his life.

The Johannine community

It is now generally recognized that behind the Johannine texts lies a community of ordinary human beings who have interpreted the story of Jesus in line with their own life experiences. Modern biblical scholarship has taken this setting seriously and has tried to reconstruct the history of the community from within which John wrote. A classic treatment of this approach has been produced by R. Brown in *The Community of the Beloved Disciple*.

Basic assumptions

In Brown's theory, the gospel of John cannot be considered in isolation from his letters since the same vocabulary and concepts appear in both. The beginning of John's first letter includes:

> We declare to you what was from the beginning, what we have heard, what we have seen with our eyes, what we have looked at and touched with our hands, concerning the word of life – this life was revealed, and we have seen it and testify to it, and declare to you the eternal life that was with the Father and was revealed to us. (1:1–2)

This is remarkably similar to the Prologue of John's gospel. There are two main ways of relating these two sources:

a) the gospel came first and the letters then comment on the approach to Jesus taken in the gospel;
b) the letters are an earlier version of the Johannine community's views, and the gospel of John represents a later editing of these.

Brown takes the first of these approaches and reconstructs the history of the Johannine community as follows.

Reconstruction and community growth

Brown claims that the influence of several generations of community growth can be seen in the gospel of John.

Firstly, there was an originating group of Jewish believers who may have had connections with John the Baptist. This would explain the high profile given to him at the start of the gospel. This group was led or strongly influenced by Jesus.

Secondly, additional members joined this group from within the Samaritan community. This accounts for the dialogue with the Samaritan woman in John 4 and the frequent references to Moses, who was specifically revered within the Samaritan tradition.

Thirdly, there would have been a stage in which the enlarged group became dissociated from the Judaism that was practised in the local synagogue. This resulted in a dislike of other Jews and led to the development within the community of a more theological understanding of Jesus.

Finally, the community is excluded entirely from the synagogue and sees the Jews as major opponents, both to itself in its developed form and also to its original founder, Jesus. Brown considers that some pagan converts may also have joined the community, but their numbers would have been small.

The effect of all this would have been to create a community which felt itself separated from both Jewish and non-Jewish society. The community saw itself as different from the world and even opposed to it. This would have meant a sectarian attitude prevailed in which the community members saw themselves as living in a 'world apart' with an identity of their own.

Separation led the group to develop an understanding about Jesus which increasingly focused on his divine origins, justifying the group's separation from society. Some members of the group would have come to see Jesus as divine and hardly human at all, whilst others would maintain an interest in the events of Jesus' life, most notably in his birth and death as these could be seen as particularly pointing to his divinity.

Eventually factional differences developed between members of the community and it fell apart. This can be traced, Brown claims, in the letters of John. These speak of the need to focus on Christ, who came in the flesh, and they attack opponents for denying this truth and denying Jesus' love commandment by disagreeing with other members of the community. The first letter of John speaks of antichrists who have appeared:

> Children, it is the last hour! As you have heard that antichrist is coming, so now many antichrists have come . . . They went out from us, but they did not belong to us; for if they had belonged to us, they would have remained with us. But by going out they made it plain that none of them belongs to us. (2:18–19)

Brown says that this points to the ultimate fate of the community – it split into two. One group took the gospel and approached the great Christian communities founded by Peter and Paul, hence the reference in John 21:18 to the leadership given to Peter. Another group took the gospel and merged with groups which were to be identified in the second and third centuries as 'Gnostics'. This accounts for the fact that the gospel of John is not mentioned in any lists of texts held by the great Christian churches until late in the second century, and yet the text seems to be assumed as the basis for a work such as the Apocryphon of John (from the Nag Hammadi texts – see Chapter 9) produced by Gnostic circles in the second century.

Brown's theory evaluated

Brown's theory expands on that of L. Martyn, who first argued for the link between the text and a community of believers. There is general agreement amongst biblical scholars that this is the right approach, but there is considerable disagreement about how much editing was involved in the gospel and therefore how many stages in community membership it reflects.

A strong note of caution to this whole line of argument has recently been registered by M. Hengel (*The Johannine Question*). Hengel argues that John should be seen as a text written directly by one of the apostles with no later editing or development. However even he has had to admit the possibility of two major stages: a text written by an apostle who was an eye-witness; and one written by an evangelist or editor who, later in the first century, recorded the oral tradition. Here, as in so many other cases in biblical scholarship, there is a multitude of theories and no agreement.

Dating John's gospel

The fourth gospel, like the other three, has no date of composition indicated within the text. Most modern scholars date John's gospel later than the Synoptics. The tradition in the early Church was that the gospel was written by the 'Beloved Disciple' (John) and this idea has recently been revived by M. Hengel in his book. However other scholars point out that there are considerable difficulties with this view (cf. p. 72).

One way of dating a document is to see whether other documents have referred to it or been influenced by it. There are no clear references to John's gospel in the writings of the early Christian Fathers before the second century (about 160–180 AD). This has led some to suggest that the gospel may have been composed as much as a hundred years after Jesus' death. However a recent papyrus fragment of John's gospel has been discovered (named as 'P^{52}') and this has been dated to the early part of the second century. It could, therefore, be that John's gospel was in existence by about 100 AD.

The sources of the gospel

As with the Synoptics, it is probable that the fourth gospel was composed from sources which were already in existence. However the nature of these sources has been the subject of considerable debate.

Rudolf Bultmann (cf. pp. 97–8, 124–5) argued that the original writer took the model for his presentation of Jesus from an existing work which made Jesus seem even more of a heavenly being than the present gospel does. The evangelist then softened this approach to show a greater awareness of Jesus' humanity. An editor then put in passages which imply ritual practices among the Johannine community. Bultmann suggested that the message about Jesus had been adapted to a Greek audience and that, therefore, the gospel belonged to a later Christian tradition than did the Synoptic gospels. However, recent investigation into first-century Judaism, especially the evidence of the Dead Sea Scrolls, have shown that the Prologue is primarily rooted in Jewish rather than Greek thought (see p. 63).

R. Fortna is a modern scholar who has investigated further the question of Johannine sources. He has worked on the basis of separating the gospel into two main sections: the Book of Signs (the miracles of Jesus), and the Book of Glory (the death of Jesus). A simple view would be that each of these two parts was originally a separate document which the evangelist wove together. It has also been argued that the discourses of Jesus were originally from a 'sayings' source, different from the sayings source which lay behind the Synoptic gospels (cf. p. 118). However there is no clear way of identifying these purported sources and no certainty is possible. The theories remain speculative

John and the Synoptics

The relation between John's gospel and the three Synoptic gospels is an obvious issue. Did the evangelist know about Matthew, Mark and Luke and did he assume that his audience knew about them as well? There is much common material in all four gospels, but there are not enough detailed texts in common to establish a link between John and any one of the other gospels. The one exception to this generalization is that there may be links between John and Luke as there does appear to be some shared material. For instance, they both have stories about Mary Magdalene. Perhaps the most likely position is that the fourth evangelist had access to stories about Jesus which formed part of a tradition which was parallel to, but separate from, the material which the writers of Matthew, Mark and Luke used.

What is more surprising is not the difference between John and the Synoptics but the remarkable degree of similarity between the two pictures of Jesus that emerge – given, as seems probable, that the gospels were written in different communities who did not share much, if any, common written material.

PART 4

SOME THEMES

In Part Two the four gospels were examined as individual stories, with their own themes and emphases. In Part Three some of the techniques of modern biblical scholarship were outlined. In this section each of the four chapters will examine parallel themes common to all four gospels. Each chapter stands on its own as the study of a particular theme and yet, at the same time, each contributes to the impression of diversity and richness of religious thought evidenced by the gospels. Four themes are investigated. The first two, miracles and parables, reflect traditional areas of research and interest in Jesus' life and his activities, but they are also topics which are of central importance in all four gospels. The second pair of themes deal with matters of more contemporary concern (women, and the concept of community/Church) and serve as good illustrations of the ways in which the gospels can be used, and abused, in contemporary debates.

THIRTEEN

The Miracle Stories

Jesus cures sickness, drives out evil spirits who are possessing individual human beings, changes water into wine, controls storms and water, and produces a huge meal from tiny resources. But these are actions pointing to something greater. They have a spiritual significance beyond the actual events recorded.

Clearly these stories were of great importance to the evangelists, but it is not so easy for a modern audience to evaluate them. One thing is clear: no one who wants to be taken seriously as a historian can simply dismiss these stories out of hand. If one believes that there is a transcendent order of reality which can overturn natural laws, then it is at least possible that one may take the miracle stories more or less literally. In the modern world, however, there is a rationalistic approach which seeks a scientific explanation for events that break the laws of nature. The philosopher Immanuel Kant wrote *Religion Within the Limits of Reason Alone* and many modern theologians follow a Kantian approach. They seek to understand the miracle stories without any suggestion of divine intervention.

David Hume holds that if one balances the evidence it is always going to be more likely that the miracle stories were fabricated or exaggerated accounts. Hume asks us to balance two possibilities:

a) that the known laws of nature are overturned as described in the gospels, or
b) that the 'ignorant and barbarous people' who contributed to the writing of the gospel stories either fabricated the stories or were influenced by their love of the unlikely or their fundamental beliefs

in evil spirits and gods to look on events as if they were breaches of nature when, in fact, they were not.

Hume maintains that it will always be more rational to accept the second of these two alternatives. (For further discussion of the philosophic issues underlying this approach see Peter Vardy's *The Puzzle of God* Chapter 17.)

G. Theissen has proposed a modern sociological perspective to miracles. He suggests that the purpose of the miracle stories is to encourage a belief that boundaries of thought and culture can be transcended and that new forms of community living can come into existence. This approach avoids the issue of what Jesus did by looking instead at the effect of the accounts on the lifestyle of a group.

Whatever view is taken on the above issue, one can certainly start by considering how the ancient world viewed the miracle stories.

The ancient worldview

In the world of the first century the prevailing belief was that God and nature were not separate realities but that they together formed the world or cosmos. God's actions interpenetrated nature. All that happened by way of fertility or drought was attributed to the gods. Human beings existed within this framework. Some supernatural activity brought advantages to human beings, some brought harm. This approach was common in the Old Testament.

At that time there was no real gap between religion and what we today might call magic. Most people today would separate the two. Many would see a value in religion but would dismiss magic. In the first century it was a punishable offence to use magic, but in practice many citizens went to private fortune-tellers and healers. Public ceremonies in the Roman Empire included divination of the future using animal entrails. For instance, in Shakespeare's play *Julius Caesar* the 'diviners' told Caesar 'not to go forth' on the Ides of

March. He refused to listen to them thus partly bringing on his death, although Brutus and his friends were also responsible. We see here an example of both 'the gods' and human beings being involved together in events.

The question for the ancient world was not 'Can miracles happen?' but rather 'Which deity or evil power brought this event about?' This is why Jesus was accused by the Pharisees of using the power of the Devil rather than God to perform miracles (see pp. 39–40). They did not dispute the miracle but they attributed the power to perform miracles to a different source.

Wonder-workers and 'men of power'

Jesus has to be seen within this first-century perspective. The gospel writers present him as in many ways like the traditional figure of a charismatic wonder-worker. In Mark 8:22 Jesus heals by using his saliva. This follows the idea that the 'mana' or inner power of a great human being could be passed on through the physical aspects of his life. It could be caught, almost like a disease. Another example of this is that those who touched the hem of Jesus' coat were healed (Matthew 14:36; Luke 8:42–6).

In other passages, however, Jesus is different from ancient wonder-workers. He does not have to use any physical means to achieve healings. In Mark 1:25–6 he commands evil spirits to leave a man and so exorcises him. Here a mere command is enough to effect the healing. Similarly, Jesus heals the centurion's servant (who may have been the centurion's batman or even, as has been suggested by some commentators, his lover) while travelling towards his house and in no physical proximity to the sick man.

However even when no physical means were used to achieve healings, there were parallels between Jesus' activity and other figures. In the Greek *Magical Papyri* (a library of magical spells and incantations found in Egypt and belonging to the period of the Roman Empire) a superior form of power is gained when a practitioner has command of a supernatural spirit whom he can rely on to work deeds of power without having to go through any complicated rituals. A mere word of power from the practitioner is all that is required.

Jesus was not, therefore, unique in having miracles and wonders attributed to him. This does not mean that he was the same as other figures, but it does mean that he was, in respect of the miracles he performed, much more similar to other figures of his time than some modern readers imagine. Of course Jesus also raised Lazarus from the dead and the gospel story maintains that he himself rose from the dead. However, even this claim is not wholly distinctive. We know that Simon Magus (a magician healed in Acts 8:9–13), was claimed to have done this as did Peter in the apocryphal text the Acts of Peter.

Signs and wonders

The evangelists do not focus simply on Jesus as a wonder-worker, rather they portray Jesus performing *signs* which make clear the wider significance of his work. John 2:11 describes Jesus' turning water into wine as 'the first sign' that he performed for his disciples, and the Synoptics have many references to Jesus' signs. Jesus not only performs signs but is also portrayed as 'the sign', as in Matthew 24:30.

. . . then the sign of the Son of man will appear in heaven . . .

Sometimes when Jesus performs a sign he is portrayed as telling the people affected not to tell anyone. He walks on water but only his own disciples see him doing so. He claims that they, too, could have done the same but did not have sufficient faith. However, in the temptation in the wilderness (Matthew 4:1–11) Jesus is depicted as refusing 'magic tricks' as a way of attracting followers. Similarly, the crowd asks for a miracle to validate Jesus' authority but he does not perform one (John 6:30); the Pharisees ask for a miracle and he refuses (Matthew 16:1–4); and Herod, after Jesus' arrest, asks him to give a sign but again he refuses (Luke 23:8–9). The only time when Jesus does give a sign to legitimate his authority is to show the validity of his word. For instance, when challenged because he forgives sins, Jesus says:

> 'Which is easier to say, "Your sins are forgiven you," or to say "Stand up and walk"? But so that you may know that the Son of Man has authority on earth to forgive sins' – he said to the one who was paralysed –, 'I say to you, stand up and take your bed and go to your home.' (Luke 5:23–5)

The point of miracles is to confirm Jesus' position as being sent by God whilst nevertheless retaining his authority. He is not a 'miracle worker' who encourages people to follow him by performing magic tricks. Jesus is shown as using God's power which works through him. He is not portrayed as working out of his own, independent human cleverness or strength.

Beelzeboul and Jesus

The three Synoptic gospels all use the story of Jesus being accused of performing wonders by the power of Beelzeboul, Prince of Demons. This accusation allows the reader to understand the universal issue at stake. (Beelzeboul is the name for the chief opponent of God, elsewhere described as Satan or the Devil.)

The NT portrays Jesus as operating in a cosmic order in which God exists with angels and archangels led by his Anointed One (Christ). The Book of Revelation, as an example, gives this picture. However God is opposed by Satan and his army of demons of unclean spirits. There is, therefore, a cosmic war in progress whose effects are experienced by human beings on earth.

In the gospels, any working of wonders is an exercise of power.

The issue is, whose power is at work? Satan and God, and their followers, can all produce wonders, but only the wonders performed by God and God's followers are really of help to human beings. As we have seen (p. 40) Jesus replies to the charge that he is using Satan's power by showing the illogicality of this approach. If he, on behalf of Satan, is opposing Satan's followers, then Satan's kingdom is at war with itself.

Power

In the NT, only the God of Israel has ultimate power. Only God, therefore, can move history forward. However the Prologue to John's gospel portrays the world as under the dominion of the powers of darkness:

> The light shines in the darkness, and the darkness did not overcome it. (John 1:5).

Again, Luke records in the temptation of Jesus in the wilderness:

> Then the devil led him up and showed him in an instant all the kingdoms of the world. And the devil said to him, 'To you I will give their glory and all this authority; for it has been given over to me, and I will give it to anyone I please. If you, then, will worship me, it will all be yours.' (Luke 4:5–7).

The world is largely in the power of the forces of evil and God's omnipotent power, although in ultimate and final control, is more manifest in weakness (which, above all, the cross represents) than in dominion and strength.

The Greek term used in the gospels for power is *dunamis*, the innate ability to act powerfully. Associated with it is another term, *exousia*. This entails a power which has been delegated to someone. The contrast between these two views of power is shown in the fourth gospel's account of Jesus' trial before Pilate. Pilate says:

> Do you refuse to speak to me? Do you not know that I have power to release you, and power to crucify you?

Jesus replies:

> You would have no power over me unless it had been given you from above . . . (John 19:10-11)

The English word for the sort of power that is being used here is 'authority' but this is different from the power attributed to Jesus. This is not random strength, it is not physical strength, it is not authority delegated from some earthly ruler. Jesus' power is portrayed as being the authority and power delegated by the God of Israel and the whole cosmos (see pp. 159, 221).

Selected miracles

There is not space in a book of this length to consider each of the miracles attributed to Jesus in depth. We have seen that other early sources attributed more unlikely 'wonders' to Jesus (cf. pp. 106–7) and that the writers of the four gospels were restrained in their choice of which stories to include. However the significance of some of the miracles is worthy of brief mention, if only because they point to the need to see each story in a wider context and not simply to regard it as an isolated piece of writing.

Feeding the 5,000
Matthew 14:13-21; Mark 6:30–44; Luke 9:10–17; John 6:1–14

This is not simply a story about how Jesus fed a large crowd with very limited resources – it is associated with a wider context. In the OT it is God who causes the crops to grow and so provides food (cf. Psalm 72). In Exodus, God miraculously sends manna and quails to feed the people of Israel when they are hungry in the desert. Through Moses' intercession, God feeds the people of Israel in their need.

Jesus as the 'new Moses' faces people in spiritual need. He will feed them ultimately through his own body and blood, symbolized by the meal shared with his disciples, but one of the signs of his power whilst on earth is that he feeds followers as Moses did. Instead of having to rely on God's power, Jesus feeds people directly through his own power thus furthering the nurturing role of God.

Walking on water/calming a storm

Matthew 14:22–33; Mark 6:45–52; John 6:15–21

In these scenes, Jesus has power over nature. He can walk on water and can quell the wind and waves. However the story is not simply to be read at this level. In Genesis 1, God creates by controlling the chaos formed by the waters. The land was formed out of the waters as a prelude to the creation of plants, animals and human beings. In creation God subdues the waters and brings order. Jesus, by walking on water, is portrayed as showing the same signs and therefore as sharing the controlling, creative force of God.

Healing Jairus' daughter

Matthew 9:18–26; Mark 5:21–43; Luke 8:40–56

Psalm 104 makes explicit an Old Testament theme: that only God can give or restore life. In 1 Kings 17 Elijah, the man of God, brings back to life a dead child through his prayer to God. Similarly, Jesus brings back to life the daughter of the synagogue's ruler. But unlike Elijah Jesus does not have to make a long prayer to God. His relationship to God is so close that he has only to reach out to the child to restore her to life. Both Elijah and Jesus demonstrate in their deeds that the God of Israel is the true God, capable of power over both life and death. They both confirm the validity of their relationship to God by God acting through them. However Jesus is superior in that he is so close to God that he can act by his own authority and not simply as an intercessor to God.

Casting out demons

Mark 1:21–7; Luke 4:31–7

In these passages, Jesus drives evil spirits out of a possessed man. The key idea being expressed here is Jesus' authority. The real wonder – which leads to Jesus' fame 'spread throughout the surrounding region of Galilee' (Mark 1:28) – is his authority over evil. The evil spirit asks:

> What have you to do with us, Jesus of Nazareth? Have you come to destroy us? I know who you are, the Holy One of God. (Mark 1:24)

It is the evil spirit who makes clear exactly who Jesus is. He is the person chosen by God, in history, to fulfil a role in the story of the universal significance of Jesus in the struggle between good and evil. Jesus represents the ultimate threat to evil, a theme to which the gospel writers constantly return. The crowds recognize this and the evangelist has them saying:

> What is this? A new teaching – with authority he commands even the unclean spirits, and they obey him! (Mark 1:27)

At the beginning of this passage Jesus is teaching in the synagogue. Again, the same theme is emphasized:

> They were astounded at his teaching, for he taught them as one having authority, and not as the scribes. (Mark 1:22)

In addition, when Jesus sent out disciples they were given authority to cast out demons (Mark 14–1). It can be seen, therefore, that Jesus' power over demons is not some 'wonder-working trick' but part of the gospel writers' wish to establish Jesus' unique authority as coming from God. When Jesus drives out evil spirits this is part of God's plan to assert his authority and to drive out from the universe the evil that now dominates it.

The miracle stories have a number of objectives but they are all intended as signs pointing to Jesus' status. Jesus is shown as having power, but this power is not simply random strength but delegated authority from God over natural and evil forces. The final miracle which provides the focus of the gospel stories is Jesus' victory over death: the belief of the Christian Church that Jesus rose from the dead as an individual; that he conquered the last great enemy, death, as well as everything that the powers of evil attempt to do in God's world.

If the possibility of events that go against the known and accepted laws of nature is rejected, then a revised understanding of the miracle stories is necessary. There are two broad approaches within this perspective: either to deny that the miracles ever happened or to attribute the miracles to Jesus' human insight or skill. Thus, he might have persuaded people to share their food in the story of the feeding of the 5,000; he might have encouraged a person to walk when they had not had the confidence to try for themselves or he might have helped people recover from epileptic fits which were attributed to the work of demon spirits.

Where the reader starts will determine where s/he ends up. Nowhere is this more the case than when considering the gospel miracle stories. If Jesus rose from the dead, then the other miracle stories are relatively minor in comparison with this event. If he did not, then Christianity may have insights into how life should be lived but, in essence, the Christian story is fictional. No amount of biblical study will settle this particular issue one way or the other.

FOURTEEN

The Parables of Jesus

Jesus performed miracles but he also taught in parables. The English word 'parable' is a translation of the Hebrew term '*mashal*'. It is not entirely clear what this word meant in its original culture setting but it may have had a connection with Jewish prophecy. Prophetic knowledge comes from a visionary experience and this can only partly be expressed in normal language. A *mashal* involves analogy, where one thing is said to be 'related' to another thing.

Parables were a well-used style of teaching in the first century. For instance, Rabbi Gamaliel II, who taught about sixty to seventy years after Jesus' death, is quoted as beginning a parable as follows: 'I will tell you a parable. With what shall I compare this? It is like an earthly king who went forth to war . . .' (Mekilta 68a, Par. Jethro. 6) Jesus began parables in a similar manner and like Gamaliel he illustrates God's activity by comparing him to an earthly king or lord (e.g. Matthew 18:23 and 22:2; Luke 14:31–2).

The shortest form of the parables occurs when Jesus says, 'The kingdom of God is like . . .' Jesus brings together two different realities: one unknown, the kingdom of God; and the other known, something in the world. He makes comparisons between them to illuminate the unknown. Jesus therefore offers an insight into God's kingdom through looking at the ordinary world with which his listeners are familiar. The following is a good example:

What is the kingdom of God like? What shall I compare it with? It is like this. A man takes a mustard seed and sows it in his field. The plant grows and becomes a tree . . . It is like this. A woman

161

takes some yeast and mixes it with forty litres of flour until the whole batch of dough rises. (Luke 13:18–21, GNB)

In each case the seed and the yeast involve the idea of a huge increase, greater than might have been expected. Thus the understanding of God's kingdom is that it, too, involves a huge expansion. Parables are not intended to be taken literally but they are intended to provide insight.

The story of the good Samaritan (Luke 10:29–37) provides an example of another type of parable. Here Jesus is asked a question, in this case: 'Who is my neighbour?' (Luke 10:29). Jesus then tells the story, followed by him returning to the question and asking, 'Who was the neighbour?' The man replies and is told by Jesus, 'Go, then, and do likewise' (Luke 10:37). This parable works on several levels. Firstly, it is a vivid story of a man beset by troubles on a journey – a common experience of the time. Secondly, it is a comment on what really constitutes holiness and purity before God. The priest and the Levite acted in accordance with the holiness code of the Old Testament and kept themselves ready to serve in the Temple (a place which, for the priest, was equivalent to God's kingdom). Yet in so doing they avoid facing their duty to their fellow human being. Thirdly, a new, provocative and scandalous view is offered. The outsider, the Samaritan, acts truly in accordance with God's will by showing love. God's kingdom, therefore, is to be found in unlikely but everyday settings. God's kingdom is less connected with institutions than with relationships of love, care, compassion and understanding between human beings. This obviously has implications for understandings of 'Church'.

The reader of the parable is invited to enter into the story. S/he is asked to make judgements about the scenes and characters being described and, in so doing, to reflect on existing values and attitudes. Parables are subversive of accepted and conventional thinking and, unlike literal descriptions, have an open-ended quality which is more complicated than at first appears.

The parables are not included simply to show what a good

teacher Jesus was. The focus of a parable lies beyond itself: in the kingdom of God. Jesus of Nazareth, it is implied, has inner understanding of the universe. Since the biblical view is that only God has power to create and change nature, it is important for human beings to understand God's purposes and intentions.

Jesus' parable style uses everyday events to reveal God's purposes. God is not totally hidden from the human mind; God is shown as loving, nurturing, caring for human beings. However the darker side of God appears as well. God is a judge and there will be a day of harvest – the end of the world – when a separation will be made between those who have chosen to follow God and those who have chosen the path of selfishness and godlessness. The final focus of many of the parables is on this eschatological event: the breaking apart of a purely human view of life through the recognition of God's plan for the future of creation.

C.H. Dodd argued that the heart of a parable is a metaphor. A metaphor uses an image of something that is familiar to talk of something which is unfamiliar. Metaphors can convey a reality which would not otherwise be accessible – they can be used to express a truth without being literally true. As an example, talk of God as a shepherd may be a helpful way of expressing truth about God but this does not mean that God is literally a human shepherd. Metaphors can also bring speech to life, can provide depth and multiple levels of understanding, and can say a great deal in a short space. Take the following example relating to football:

> Arsenal are four-nil down to Madrid – there's a vacuum in defence, they're all at sea in midfield and they've got a mountain to climb up front!

No one, but no one, would read this and think literally of vacuums, seas and mountains. Instead, these are vivid images which conjure up an entire game in a single sentence. Parables have a similar function, and although more than one understanding is possible, a truth is clearly being expressed. In our example, Arsenal are clearly losing,

Madrid is dominating the play, the defence and mid-field play is disastrous and the forwards are facing a near-impossible task. This literal analysis fails to capture the reality of the metaphor, but it shows that the original sentence is claiming to capture a truth. The same applies to the use of metaphors in the Bible.

The use of parables can bring the reader to see something of God's purpose in the world. However parables do need to be understood, and one of the problems with them is that their meaning is not always clear. If, for instance, God is regarded as a father or a landowner, then clearly God is not a human father or a human landowner. Even if these words are understood metaphorically, there are problems with understanding what it means, say, to talk to God as Father. In today's world, with many cases of fathers beating and sexually abusing children and with many women being aware of the negative images conjured up by a male image of God, talk of God as Father may be distinctly unhelpful. Interpreting parables can, similarly, be difficult.

Sometimes explanations are given of what the parables in the gospels mean, but whether these interpretations are given by Jesus or by the evangelists is impossible to determine. At the least, however, they provide guidance as to how the parables were understood by near contemporaries of Jesus. This is important and is, perhaps, the nearest one can come to 'truth' by means of literary analysis.

Sources of the parables

Parables provide a vivid and dynamic teaching medium but, as with Jesus' miracles, the question has to be raised: Were all the parables related to Jesus? No certainty is possible, but in general terms the spontaneity of the parable stories fits with the general picture given of Jesus in the gospels. Most of the parables draw on scenes from life in first-century Palestine or on biblical tradition. As an example, the parable of the vineyard draws on the image of Israel as God's vine.

All this is in keeping with seeing Jesus as an itinerant Jewish teacher. It may also be that Jesus used 'local news' as a basis for teaching. The parable of the unjust steward (Luke 16:1–8) could be an example of this. Perhaps the disciples were discussing a local case of injustice and then Jesus used their discussion as the foundation for relaying his own ideas.

This same parable, however, shows the modern reader some of the difficulties of being certain about what it was that Jesus said. The story unfolds until it comes to a surprising verse:

> . . . the master of this dishonest manager praised him for doing such a shrewd thing; because the people of this world are much more shrewd in handling their affairs than the people who belong to the light. (Luke 16:8, GNB)

This seems to indicate that Jesus is commending 'worldly' shrewdness as opposed to honesty and straight dealing. Is the 'master' referred to here part of the story or does the parable refer to Jesus commending his followers for using dishonest means?

Immediately after this verse there is material which is clearly intended as a commentary on the fuller meaning of the previous text:

> And so I tell you; make friends for yourselves with worldly wealth, so that when it gives out, you will be welcomed in the eternal home. (Luke 16:9, GNB).

The connection between this comment and the previous parable is far from clear. It may have been that this was a later saying attributed to Jesus which was inserted at this point. There is certainly a lack of unity in this material. Which material came from Jesus: which was attributed to Jesus by one of the early Christian communities and which was inserted by the evangelist is a matter of conjecture.

A further example of the problem of interpretation occurs immediately after the above material. Jesus is recorded as saying:

No servant can be the slave of two masters; either he will hate one and love the other; or he will be loyal to one and despise the other. You cannot serve both God and mammon. (Luke 16:13).

The 'mammon' referred to here may be anything futile in which an individual trusts for security. Putting trust in something means being committed to it. To the modern reader it may seem 'obvious' that Jesus was saying that an individual should only be committed to one thing – to God. However this may not have been the meaning of the original parable. Two things could have happened:

a) Jesus could have told the parable in Luke 16:1–8 and offered the other sayings at different times. The editor may then have put the different material together.

b) Jesus could have told the parable and then Christian preaching could have given rise to the other teachings which expounded the parable for a new audience and these teachings then came to be attributed to Jesus. For instance, in the parable of the sower and the seed (Mark 4:1–20) J. Jeremias regarded verses 10–20 as being added at a later date to explain the parable.

Both the above approaches are possible and it is likely that the gospels record a mixture of the two.

All the gospels include examples of Jesus teaching by means of parables, but Luke has by far the greatest number. Was this because the tradition that Luke used had more parables in it? Was it because Luke felt freer to add to the stories available to him because he thought that this was in the tradition of Jesus? There is no way of answering these questions.

Purpose of the parables

Adolf Julicher, C.H. Dodd and J. Jeremias saw the parables as stories with one or more 'message'. Thus the task of the scholar is to uncover the original message of Jesus, free from the additions by the evangelists. Perhaps, however, this is a mistaken approach and the understanding of parables has to be sought at a different level.

Paul Ricoeur argues that the gospel parables break through convention:

> The parable surprises, astonishes, shocks, provokes: exposing such and such a prejudgment (an opinion or belief imposed by one's milieu, one's education or the epoch), it obliges one to reconsider things, to come to a new decision. (*The Kingdom*, p. 166)

Jesus, surprisingly, says that the parables are not intended to reveal truth but to make understanding more difficult. Speaking to his disciples he says:

> To you has been given the secret of the kingdom of God, but for those outside, everything comes in parables; in order that they may indeed look, but not perceive, and may indeed listen, but not understand, so that they may not turn again and be forgiven. (Mark 4:11–12).

In *The Scandal of the Gospels* (OUP , 1994) David McCracken argues that the parables were intended by Jesus as stumbling blocks to his hearers. They confronted people and enabled them to hear the parables either as lies or as truth. People's attitudes to the parables would be determined by the desires they revealed.

The parable of the vineyard labourers (Matthew 20:1–16) is sometimes used by capitalists as support for free enterprise. It is held to indicate that the owner was in his rights to pay as he pleased. This interpretation leaves the status quo intact; it is non-threatening and non-challenging. However other interpretations are open. As McCracken says:

> . . . among the characters [in the parable] is a potentially signifi-

cant transformation which is left unresolved. I refer to the twelve-hour workers who are transformed into grumblers, offended at what they take to be unjust treatment. 'These last worked only one hour' they say 'and you have made them equal to us who have borne the burden of the day and the scorching heat'. They receive an explanation, likely to be unsatisfactory, and are told to 'Take what belongs to you and go' and are left with the choice of being envious because of the landowner's generosity (seeing self-proclaimed goodness with an evil eye) or not. They may choose to remain offended or not, but the reasons offered for not being offended are, by normal standards, not compelling. (p. 78)

McCracken is arguing that Jesus' message is scandalous, that it is likely to result in offence and to be rejected. It is not 'sensible', it is not 'rational', it is apparent foolishness.

The parable of the forgiving king and the unforgiving slave (Matthew 18:21–35) provides another example:

. . . the debt [forgiven by the king] is the equivalent of roughly ten million dollars. The king's first impulse, when the slave was brought to him, is to sell the slave, his wife, his children and his possessions, since the slave could not repay the money . . . the king does not accede to [the slave's] request, that he be patient, but instead cancels the debt of ten million dollars. He does this 'out of pity' and for no other reason . . . It is an extreme, unworldly, unexpected, un-asked-for, nearly unthinkable and certainly irrational act of forgiveness. And undeserved . . . (p. 124)

The kingdom of heaven is not something that can be readily understood, as if one was learning the facts in a geography lesson about another country. It may mean dying to a normal way of understanding, being willing to accept apparent contradictions and being unable to grasp the content firmly. It may involve living with ambiguity and lack of clarity.

The parables present people with choices as to how they will react. They challenge people's preconceptions and invite a radical response. This response will be transforming, or it will result in the parable being rejected or reinterpreted in the service of self-interest and the status quo. Many of the parables are left open-ended and this is because the ending is provided by the reader's interpretations. Ernst Fuchs says that the parables demand a decision:

> . . . like the man who found the treasure, or the pearl merchant who found the one pearl of great price, the hearer must stake all on one thing – that he can win the future that Jesus proclaims to him . . . It is up to the person who understands the parable to give the verdict on the truth of Jesus' claim. It is the person who understands who has to decide. (quoted in McCracken, p. 87).

Parables, therefore, may be more sophisticated than many modern commentators who rest content with literary analysis may allow. They may be sophisticated devices, used by Jesus himself, to confront people and to reveal to them something about themselves. They may offend people and drive them away from seeing God in Jesus, or they may confront them and demand a response. If this diversity of interpretation is indeed present, then there is no single 'meaning' to be given to the parables. The meaning is intimately bound up with the reader and the reader's response. There may be more going on in the parables than the self-centred individual may be able to see.

FIFTEEN

Women in the Gospels

Throughout the history of Christianity, there have been frequent times when Christian Churches, governments and individuals have systematically persecuted the Jews. There are, of course, passages in certain of the gospels which imply that the Jewish leaders were responsible for Jesus' death. This has been used as a pretext, but it is only a pretext. Jesus was himself a Jew and there is no evidence whatsoever which would support this way of using Jesus' message.

Much the same position occurs in the case of women. Throughout Christian history women have been subjugated and 'kept in their place' by the Christian Church. Still today the Roman Catholic and Orthodox Churches refuse to ordain women. More seriously, the history of the Christian Church has been a largely male-dominated history, where the feminine perspective has been denied or suppressed. To be sure, there were occasional instances of great women figures in the life of the Church – Hildegard of Bingen, Catherine of Siena, Julian of Norwich, Teresa of Avila, Mary Ward, Evelyn Underhill, Simone Weil and others – but these have been in a distinct minority. To an extent, this subjugation of women's role continued a tradition present in first-century Palestine and still present in many societies in the world today.

In both pagan and Jewish society women were considered to be less intelligent than men. Whereas male children needed a guardian until they came of age, women were held to always need a male guardian since they were considered to have no head for business and to be unable to manage their own affairs. There were, in practice, some variations on this theme. The status and power of women would have been different according to the social class they belonged to, and in the home both Roman and Jewish women had a decisive role. However in the wider arena of social life, in politics and religious affairs, women has almost no role at all.

Just as Christians misapplied Jesus' essential message to the Jews, similarly Christian Churches and individuals have done the same to women. Jesus' own teachings, as recorded in the gospels, give no warrant whatsoever for this approach.

In the New Testament as a whole there are references to twenty-nine women, as well as references to groups of women such as those who accompanied Jesus and his followers. The Acts of the Apostles refers to a number of women who played key roles in the missionary activity of early Christianity – women such as Damaris (Acts 17:34) or Priscilla (Act 18:2ff), of whom it is said:

Now there came to Ephesus a Jew named Apollos, a native of Alexandria. He was an eloquent man, well versed in the scriptures. He had been instructed in the way of the Lord, and he spoke with burning enthusiasm and taught accurately things concerning Jesus, although he knew only the Baptism of John . . . When Priscilla and Aquila heard him they took him aside and explained the way of God to him more accurately. (Acts 18:24–6)

In Paul's letters, also, there are references to women as co-workers, including a reference to a church leader called Phoebe:

I commend to you our sister Phoebe, a deaconess of the church at Cenchreae, so that you may welcome her in the Lord as is fitting for the saints, and help her in whatever she may require from you, for she has been a great benefactor of many, and myself as well. Greet Priscilla and Aquila, who work with me in Jesus Christ and who risked their necks for my life, to whom not only I give thanks, but also all the churches of the Gentiles . . . Greet Mary, who has worked very hard among you. (Romans 16:1–6).

It is made quite clear that the 'good news' about Jesus appealed equally to men and women. Thus:

> According to his usual habit, Paul went to the synagogue . . . quoting and explaining the scriptures . . . some of them were convinced and joined Paul and Silas; so did many of the leading women. (Acts 17:2–4, GNB)

> The People [at Berea] were more open-minded than the people in Thessalonica. They listened to the message with great eagerness . . . Many of them believed, and many Greek women of high social standing and many Greek men also believed. (Acts 17:11–12, GNB)

Why did women attach themselves to the early Christian Church?

Women and Jesus' teaching

Given that Jesus lived in a world dominated by men and, in particular, that Jewish approaches to religion were male-dominated, the approach taken to women in the gospels could hardly provoke a greater contrast. Throughout the gospels the position of women is affirmed. Examples include:

1. The angel Gabriel comes to Mary and it is Mary, an unmarried mother-to-be, who is shown as the key symbol of obedience to God's will. In the same way, Elizabeth (mother of John the Baptist) names her newborn child John – taking the initiative and providing the opportunity for her husband's disbelief to be forgiven and for him to be allowed to speak again (Luke 1:59–64).
2. It is Anna, a prophetess who did not leave the Temple in Jerusalem and worshipped and prayed night and day, who was the first to talk of Jesus to 'all who were looking for the redemption of Jerusalem' (Luke 2:36–8).

3. Jesus talks to women even though they are outcasts – much to the surprise of his disciples, as he was offending all the normal conventions (cf. John 4:27).

4. The people who are offended by Jesus (cf. pp. 215–19) are always men – the scribes and Pharisees. Jesus' forgiveness, healing and mercy, by contrast, come to both women and men equally.

5. At the cross it is the women who followed Jesus from Galilee and who looked after him (Matthew 27:55–6); women who noted where his body was laid and prepared spices and ointments for it (Luke 23:55–6); and women who came first to the tomb to see to the proper funeral rites (Matthew 28:1). In John's gospel, Mary Magdalene is the first witness to be at the tomb and to bring the news to the disciples that the stone had been rolled away (John 20:1). Mary called Peter and 'the disciple whom Jesus loved' (John 20:2). They went into the tomb, but it was she who saw the two angels in the tomb who talked to her (John 20:11–13). Mary was also the first to see and speak to the risen Jesus (John 20:14–16). Mary Magdalene's first reaction is clearly to give Jesus a hug, but Jesus tells her:

> Do not hold me, because I have not yet ascended to the Father. But go to my brothers and say to them, I am ascending to my Father and your Father, to my God and your God. (John 20:17)

Jesus also meets the needs of sick and troubled women on numerous occasions. In general, Jesus shows an openness to these women. He is not afraid to be touched by a ritually unclean woman who is suffering from a haemorrhage. (A woman was regarded as being unclean when she had a period, a position based on the holiness teaching of Leviticus and still advanced by some conservative scholars as a reason why women should not be allowed to officiate at the altar.) Jesus' personal power turns the woman's marginalized position into that of a fully recognized human being with the right to stand inside the community of faith. In other examples, Jesus heals Jairus' young daughter and, unlike everyone else, refuses to condemn the woman who was caught while committing adultery – under Jewish Law, punishable by

being stoned to death (John 8:3–11). Jesus releases her from the possibility of this death but, more than that, his response shows the
hypocrisy of the male accusers by commanding, 'Let the one who is
without sin cast the first stone.' The implication is clear: all human
beings are sinners and the woman is not to be treated as a scapegoat.

Jesus has close and intimate relationships with women. He allows
a woman to wash his feet and wipe them with her hair (John 12:3)
and claims that this woman, Mary, will be remembered for ever for
her faith in him. Jesus had a close bond with the family at Bethany.
When Lazarus died Jesus was moved to tears when he saw the
distress of Lazarus' sisters (John 11:5–44). At the same time, Mary
and Martha both demonstrate a strength and confidence in Jesus
which leads to Lazarus' resurrection. Mary says:

> Lord, if you had been there, my brother would not have died.
> (John 11:32)

Yet for all the evidence of his involvement with and concern for
women, Jesus called twelve disciples to follow him and these were
all male. This has to be recognized with regard to the position held
by the Roman Catholic Church's Magisterium and by the
Orthodox Church: that Jesus was being gender-specific in his call,
thus priests have to be male. Any suggestion that there could be
even discussion about the possibility of future female Catholic
priests has been condemned by the Magisterium as something no
Catholic scholar should contemplate. A further argument in favour
of this position is that Jesus was a man so a male priest is needed to
represent him at the altar.

However, it is not easy to be sure of Jesus' own intentions and yet
it is all too easy to apply our own preconceptions to Jesus' reported
words and actions. The Catholic Church's position is clearly one
possibility, but an alternative is to say that Jesus was a human being as
well as being God, and the priest before the altar is a human being
representing Jesus to other human beings. In this case, the gender of
the priest would be irrelevant.

The call to discipleship may well have reflected the conventions prevailing in first-century society. Sending out women to preach might not have been effective or acceptable. On this understanding, women as well as men could be Christian leaders (as the Acts of the Apostles makes clear was the case in the early Church). No certainty is possible by simply looking at the gospel texts. Here, as elsewhere, particular interpretations of the gospel passages may tell us more about the people or organizations putting forward these interpretations than about Jesus' own position. As on other issues, there is ambiguity and room for diversity of interpretation.

Mary, the mother of Jesus

Mary, Jesus' mother, is also a key figure in the gospel accounts – not just in Jesus' birth and upbringing but again at his death, when he shows his care for her (John 19:26–7). In the Christian Church Mary has traditionally been portrayed as the 'obedient little woman at home', doing what she is told by the men, passive and self-effacing. However it is just as easy and rather more persuasive to stress Mary's resourcefulness and courage. She agreed to accept Jesus' birth and to be obedient to God's will while knowing well that this would place her in a position of being a social outcast. Far from staying at home she embarks on three demanding journeys: firstly to visit her cousin Elizabeth in Jerusalem where she stayed for three months (Luke 1:56); then to accompany Joseph whilst she was in an advanced state of pregnancy (Luke 2:4–5); and finally she sets off, with Joseph and the newborn baby, to Egypt (Matthew 2:13–15).

Mary is often portrayed in Church teaching as a 'perpetual virgin' – in other words, that she never made love to Joseph. This enabled the Church to portray her as a 'woman apart', a married virgin: a difficult role model for most women. The gospel evidence for this position is non-existent. To be sure, Mary is not recorded as sleeping with Joseph before Jesus was born:

> When Joseph awoke from sleep, he did as the angel of the Lord commanded him; he took her as his wife, but had no marital relations with her until she had borne a son . . . (Matthew 1:24–5)

There is a clear implication here of normal sexual activity after the birth of Jesus. What is more, the gospels refer to Jesus having brothers:

> Then his mother and his brothers came to him, but they could not reach him because of the crowd. And he was told, 'Your mother and your brothers are standing outside, wanting to see you.' But he said to them, 'My mother and my brothers are those who hear the word of God and do it.' (Luke 8:19–21)

James is also described as 'the Lord's brother' on a number of occasions, including in the epistles (e.g. Galatians 1:19). In the Synoptics Jesus is dismissed by the crowd who say:

> Is not this the carpenter, the son of Mary and brother of James and Joses and Judas and Simon, and are not his sisters here with us? (Mark 6:3; Matthew 13:55–6)

The Church has held that such passages did not mean that Jesus really had brothers or sisters – they were spiritual relationships, or else 'brother' could refer to any close relative such as a cousin. Certainly the sense of the texts, particularly Luke 8:19–21, implies that Jesus is precisely making the point that his *real* mother and brothers are those who do God's will, not those to whom he happens to be related by ties of blood.

No certainty on the issue of Mary's sexual status is possible, but if anything the gospel texts appear to support the picture of an extraordinarily brave, resourceful and faithful woman. She was also a normal wife and mother who made love to her husband, like any other woman, after the birth of Jesus.

Women, the feminine and inclusiveness

As well as studying the role of women characters in the gospel stories, questions can be asked about the feminine aspect of human personality in the gospel stories. E. Schüssler-Fiorenza in *In Memory of Her* has suggested that one important aspect of Jesus' approach is his inclusive attitude towards the feminine dimension of humanity. This was one of the hallmarks of the early Christian Church which set it apart from Judaism at the time. Jesus engages with the marginalized people in society and one of these groups, alongside tax collectors and other sinners, is prostitutes. This class of women usually consists of the economically poorest of women who subsist by selling their own bodies for use by men. Jesus takes these women and brings them into God's kingdom. The message for women in general, and the feminine side in particular, is not condemnation and rejection but inclusion.

The same is true, in a more abstract way, with the theology of Wisdom. C.V. Camp in *The Feminine in the Book of Proverbs* points out that the 'wise woman' in Proverbs 31, who nurtures and cares for her household and who is full of gracious goodness and care for all those around her, is a symbol not just of living wisely but also of the nature of Wisdom itself. It is an image of God's divine, nurturing care. In the gospels, particularly in Matthew, Jesus is associated with divine Wisdom. The yoke which Jesus offers is like the yoke of discipline which the lady Wisdom offers in Proverb 1:

> Wisdom cries out in the street, in the squares she raises her voice, at the busiest corner she cries out, at the entrance of the city gates she speaks . . . 'I have called and you refused, have stretched out my hand and no one heeded . . .' (Proverbs 1:20–21, 24)

Schüssler-Fiorenza has suggested in her study that Jesus' Wisdom is like God's Wisdom in Proverbs: having the power to attract women in their ordinary, daily lives whilst integrating the feminine with the masculine in images of God.

Jesus breaks down the barriers between 'inside' and 'outside' and calls all human beings into God's kingdom: slave and free person, Jew and Gentile, young and old, male and female. The gospel message seems to be that in God's kingdom all distinctions imposed by human society are abolished.

SIXTEEN

Jesus, Community and Church

Commentators who write about the gospels sometimes refer to the Christian 'Church'. They often assume that the term means the same in first-century Christianity as it does today and tend to understand the first-century texts in terms of modern ideas. As an example, they assume the existence of an institutional Church from the first century onwards and sometimes argue that Jesus came to found such a Church and that new Christians were knowingly assimilated into that institution. This Church was the 'new Israel' and it was in the Church that Jesus saw salvation being found. This view is contrary to the evidence.

So where does the 'modern view' come from? We have already seen that the second part of Luke's gospel is the Acts of the Apostles. This book focuses on the growth of Christian communities and records the beginning of a 'worldwide' network quickly growing up in the first century. This is the view of the writer of Luke/Acts who, although quite close to the events he wrote about, is himself looking back in time. In addition to the Acts of the Apostles, there are the letters of Paul to individual churches (e.g. 'The church of the saints in . . .') Unreflective use of evidence such as this has led some commentators on Christianity to overlook the rather different evidence found in the gospels.

Church, movement or community?

It is true that, from the start, Jesus gathered round him a number of followers who accompanied him on his journeys. There is clear evidence of this in the gospels. However it is when one looks at the issues more deeply that the varieties of approaches set out in the gospels become apparent.

Some modern scholars tend to use the term 'movement' ('the Jesus movement') rather than 'Church' to describe the social grouping around Jesus. However the term 'movement' is rather too vague as there are signs in the gospels of a much closer-knit community than this implies. 'Community' might be a better word. In a community there is a sense of belonging to a group with its own social boundaries but without a fixed, established order. It must be remembered, however, that the first Christians were Jews. Judaism already had its own well-established institutions, including the Temple; an established form of worship; a sacred calendar; social laws; and synagogues scattered around the Roman Empire. There was no immediate need for Jesus or his followers to create new structures – the Jewish structure was perfectly adequate for Jesus' ministry. Jesus offered his contemporaries, though, a new way of interpreting the old. Indeed Jesus' teaching can be seen as a renewal of or reform within Judaism. Jesus was a member of the Jewish community and so were his followers; they worshipped in the synagogues and saw themselves as Jews – only gradually did they come to form a separate identity.

The most appropriate term for those who recognized Jesus as coming from God and who came together to form early communities may be 'the followers of Jesus' or 'disciples of Jesus'. The term 'disciple' comes from Pharisaic Judaism in which each Teacher had a following of disciples who studied his thought. This is the term used by Matthew and also by John in their gospels. These disciples, these 'followers', were, eventually, to coalesce into the Christian Church – but this took some time.

The early, early Church

The term 'early Church' is generally used to refer to the Christian Church in the first few centuries after Jesus' death. However in the thirty or forty years when the gospel material was being collected and written down there was no such thing as a clearly defined Church.

The picture that emerges in the Acts of the Apostles is of a group of Jesus' followers, increasing in number, centred on Jerusalem and led by some of the original disciples. Paul, by contrast, was out 'on the road' travelling and spreading the news about Jesus. It would be wrong to rely too heavily on the historical accuracy of Acts. This book was written some time after the events and clearly was written by someone who thought highly of Paul. The motives of the compiler of Acts are not clear and no certainty is possible about the accuracy of the events described. However Acts provides the only record we have, apart from Paul's letters, about the development of the early Christian communities.

Acts records differences of opinion arising as to whether new followers of Jesus had to be part of the Jewish community or not. At first, the followers of Jesus in each city would have been Jews, but Jesus' message appealed to Gentiles as well. Small groups of followers met in people's houses initially. Many cities developed communities of followers and these began to be called 'churches' (hence Paul writes to 'The church of the Thessalonians' or to 'The church of God which is at Corinth'). But these churches were independent from each other, often held together by loyalty to their founder – notably Paul. Paul's letters are attempts to exert his influence on these groups when he was away from them (for instance, 1 Corinthians 4:14–8:13), and he sometimes speaks on his own authority. Paul was at pains to point out, however, that the loyalty of the churches should not be to him but to the risen Christ in whom the new Christians believed.

An inevitable clash arose between Paul and the Jerusalem-based Christians about the status of new followers: did they have to become Jews by being circumcised and obeying the Jewish food laws? Paul went to Jerusalem to meet the leaders of that community to sort the matter out. Acts 15 sets out the background to and consequences of this meeting. Some of the more conservative elements in the Jerusalem church insisted that new followers had to be Jews (Acts15:5), but finally, after debate, it was decided that the

Christian movement should be open to all – it should have its own identity and there was no need for new followers of Jesus to also be Jews (Acts 15:19–21).

This was a decisive moment in the spread of Jesus' message. It opened the door to the formation of a Christian Church with its own structures, its own worship and its own organization – independent from the Jewish synagogue. The date of the Council of Jerusalem, the first Council in the history of the Christian Church, has been suggested as 49 AD, some sixteen years after Jesus' crucifixion (the date of which can only be fixed approximately). Immediately after the Jerusalem Council Acts records messages being sent to the communities founded by Paul proclaiming the new agreement. This is the first indication of a single authority being exerted over Jesus' new followers. It is likely that this authority would have increased with the passage of time and clearly the gathering in Jerusalem would have been important in bringing together stories about Jesus' life and death.

The Jerusalem church would have retained a commitment to Jewish practice and to Temple worship until the Temple was destroyed in 70 AD. We do not know for certain what the organization of the Jerusalem church was like, although it appears to have been a well-ordered community. Peter and James are recorded in Acts as having leading roles. Jerusalem was destroyed in 70 AD so by then the 'home' church would have moved to Rome, which was the centre of the Roman Empire. Exactly when this move took place is not clear.

Travel around the Roman Empire was easy and swift so communications would have been good. Travellers from one community would have been sure of a welcome in others. Local centres of Jesus' followers would have arisen, particularly in cities like Antioch, Athens, Collossos, Ephesus, Laodicea, Pergamum, Smyrna, Corinth and, of course, Rome. However it would have been some considerable time before Rome became the acknowledged centre of the diverse communities of Christian followers.

The Roman church Community has been linked to Paul (whom Acts records as being taken prisoner to Rome) and also to Peter, both of whom are held to have been martyred there. The Roman church, therefore, had an authority which was based on eye-witness accounts and also looked to the two great figures of the early years after Jesus' death. This is certainly the impression gained from the work of the fourth-century church historian Eusebius, and it is very likely to have been historically accurate. As Christianity grew so the authority of the Roman centre would have grown as well, but this was a long process, measured in hundreds of years. It is, therefore, anachronistic to project back in time the idea that there was a clearly developed 'Church' present in the first century. This was something that only gradually developed.

The gospel evidence

The term for Church, *ekklesia*, is only used twice in the gospels, on both occasions in Matthew. Crucial to one's understanding of how 'Church' is understood is the interpretation of the following quotation about Peter. (John's gospel also records the reference to Simon Peter as a rock.):

> And I tell you, you are Peter, and on this rock I will build my church, and the gates of Hades will not prevail against it. I will give you the keys of the kingdom of heaven, and whatever you bind on earth will be bound in heaven, and whatever you loose on earth will be loosed in heaven. (Matthew 16:18–19)

The second Matthean reference to 'Church' is:

> If another member of the church sins against you, go and point out the fault when the two of you are alone . . . if you are not listened to, take one or two others along with you . . . if the member refuses to listen to them, tell it to the church; and if the offender refuses to listen even to the church, let such a one be to you as a Gentile and a tax collector. (Matthew 18:15–17)

The main interpretations regarding these Matthean passages are as follows:

1. Jesus said these words and intended to form a new organizational body which Peter and his successors would lead. The Roman Catholic Church takes this position. There is no clear evidence in the text for Peter having successors who would take over his position, although it is a possibility.

2. Jesus said these words and intended Peter to lead his followers. Either Jesus may have expected the end of the world to come soon after his death (as some commentators suggest), or the words may have applied to Peter's role for his lifetime alone. The 'end of the world' expectation by Jesus is evidenced by texts such as Jesus' sending out disciples throughout Israel (seventy are sent out in Luke, whereas in Matthew it is the twelve apostles). Jesus says to them:

> . . . truly, I tell you, you will not have gone through all the towns of Israel before the Son of man comes. (Matthew 10:23)

3. The community within which Matthew's gospel was written may have looked to Peter as its leader. The first passage may have been inserted to legitimate this leadership whilst the second may have been intended to emphasize the power of the church authorities to regulate disputes. The power of 'binding and loosing', used in reference to Peter, may refer to the legal authority within the community. If this was the case, Peter's actual role would have been limited. Matthew contains no indication of a tightly structured church organization or set of doctrines apart from what Judaism already offered. There are, however, references in Matthew to disputes among Jesus' followers and these were to be settled within a set structure.

The third option is the most likely, although no certainty is possible.

It does seem unlikely that Jesus, who broke down the barriers between 'insiders' and 'outsiders' and who mixed with sinners and tax collectors, should then turn round and instruct his followers to ostracize individuals as if they were 'Gentiles and tax collectors'. The early Christian community, on the other hand, would have had good reason to attribute these sayings to Jesus to emphasize its authority.

It is important to recognize that even though the term 'Church' is used in Matthew it would not have had the same weight as in the twentieth century. The Matthean community, as it appears in the gospel, is still a loosely structured organization. There are key authority figures but without them any group would founder. These Christians were still in the process of moving into a new identity, separate from Judaism.

Jesus came to call individuals to follow him, but he also saw his followers as the 'new Israel'. He, like John the Baptist, baptized people and this may have been the mark of initiation into the new community. Thus in Acts 10:47–8 Peter agrees to baptize Gentiles after they have already received the Holy Spirit.

Jesus' followers were called on to 'love one another' and Jesus clearly saw them being bound together in opposition to the world. It was out of this understanding that groups of followers came together and the early Christian Church gradually evolved. However there is little warrant in the gospels to confirm or deny claims about the status of the whole Christian Church or individual denominational churches in the modern world.

PART 5

THE QUESTION OF TRUTH

SEVENTEEN

Biblical Language and Truth

Biblical language

The idea that words have a fixed meaning has long been displaced: meaning depends on use, as Wittgenstein made clear. Take the word 'gay'. To say 'This man is gay' meant something entirely different fifty years ago from the meaning it has today. Language is dynamic, it evolves over time, and meaning and usage vary. One cannot, therefore, just assume that the way writers 1,900 years ago used words is the same as our usage today. And it is not just individual words whose meanings change. The gospels use metaphors, similes and allegories and to understand these one has to understand the connotations and references implied within the expressions. To say that 'God is a living fire', 'God is my rock' or 'God is our Father' may convey truth without being literally true. Such language uses helpful pictures and images, and the gospel story may be functioning in this way.

Every word of the gospels cannot be true in a straightforward sense – the gospels were never intended to be read in this way. In a number of cases different gospels give flatly varying accounts. The timing of the last meal Jesus had with his disciples (pp. 72–3), the length of his ministry or the dating of Jesus' cleansing of the Temple (which in John 2:5 appears right at the beginning of Jesus' ministry and in the Synoptics is at the end, as in Luke 19:45–6) are but three examples.

The claim that the gospel writers were not interested in writing 'history', as we now understand the term, and that they took no account of the events that actually occurred will not stand up to serious scrutiny. The differences between the gospel stories point to their arising within different Christian communities. Yet in spite of these differences in development and emphasis there is remarkable agreement in the different accounts.

Truth in the gospels

Talk of 'truth' is not straightforward, yet truth matters. John's gospel more than any other takes truth seriously. At various times throughout the gospel Jesus says, 'I am the way, the *truth* and the life' – in other words, claiming that truth resides in Jesus' life and not simply in facts about Jesus. This is a different view of truth to that normally adopted, which is related to statements. Jesus also frequently indicates important statements by saying '*Truly* I say to you . . .' (In more traditional versions of the Bible this is translated 'Verily I say unto you . . .') In one of the most significant passages of the gospel, Jesus says to Pilate:

> For this I was born, and for this I came into the world, to testify to the *truth*. Everyone who belongs to the truth listens to my voice. (18:37)

Pilate replies with three words of great significance:

> What is *truth*? (18:38)

Finally, the author of John's gospel makes a specific claim to be writing the truth:

> This is the disciple who is testifying to these things and has written them, and we know that his testimony is *true*. (21:24)

John's gospel claims that Jesus *was* the truth – his life represented the truth. The absurdity of Pilate's question, and the irony implicit in the way John presents the story, is that it is addressed to Jesus who

190

was the truth. Confronted with this truth, represented by God's Word becoming a human being, Pilate fails to recognize it and instead ponders a general philosophic issue about the abstract nature of truth.

If, then, the gospels themselves recognize the complexity of talking about truth, it should be clear that what it means for the gospel stories to be true is not going to be straightforward. Yet the issue of truth matters. Those who dedicate their lives to Jesus and who call themselves Christians stake their faith on the accuracy of the gospel stories. However, as we have seen, these stories are not straightforward. Is Christian faith therefore built on weak ground?

It might be better not to ask 'Are the gospels false or true?', but to re-phrase the question and to ask 'Is the gospel story true?' The answer to this depends on a preliminary question: 'Is there a single gospel story?' This book would appear at first sight to count against there being any single narrative, although such an inference would be mistaken. The differences between the accounts attributed to Matthew, Mark, Luke and John and even to some of the apocryphal material (see pp. 104–8) may have more to do with the theological glosses put on the story by the different writers than with differences of substance. After all, the gospel writers were human beings, putting together stories about Jesus from various sources.

The old, old story

A well-known hymn by Katherine Hankey includes these lines:

Tell me the old, old story
Of Jesus and his love . . .

There is such an 'old, old story' and nothing in current biblical scholarship necessarily undermines it. The essentials of the gospel story would be as readily agreed by Christians today as they would have been 1,800 years ago. Then, as today, there would have been disputes about some of the details but the early Christians might well have been more at home with such disputes than are their modern equivalents, some of whom wish to affirm certainties which leave no room for ambiguities. The early Christians lived in a world where the apocryphal gospels circulated, and in the first century there was no agreed text. It is not as if we have moved from a golden age of clarity in the early years to confusion now. Having said that, it is not easy to arrive at a simple summary of what 'the gospel story' is.

In the next chapter a start will be made on looking at the essentials of this story. The examination will be made in stages, trying to identify the key points on which the issue of truth depends – as it might have appeared to one of Jesus' near contemporaries or, in much the same way, how it might appear to an interested individual today.

EIGHTEEN

God and Jesus

Stage one

God

God lies at the heart of the gospel story. If one lived in first century Israel then the existence of God would have been almost unquestioned. There was a general assumption among all Jews that God existed and exerted a providential care over his chosen people, Israel. Today this assumption is widely rejected and the gospel story is then looked at from this starting point. Clearly the assumption of the non-existence of God will have a radical effect on how the gospel material is to be understood.

If God does not exist and if he did not create and does not sustain the universe, then the whole of the gospel story is essentially false. There would be no miracles seen as a breach of the presently understood laws of nature, no resurrection; nor could Jesus be in a unique relationship to God as there would not be any God with whom one could be in relationship. This may seem obvious, but it is frequently the differing attitude of scholars to this key question that determines how they react to the remainder of the gospel story. The a priori assumptions brought to any reading of the gospels often tells one more about the reader than about the events.

In 1964 the Roman Catholic Biblical Commission issued a long statement regarding the historical truth of the gospels and how Catholic scholars should address the documents. One paragraph in this statement read as follows:

Some proponents [of biblical criticism] have been led astray by the prejudiced views of rationalism. They refuse to admit the existence of a supernatural order and the intervention of a personal God in the world . . . and the possibility and existence of miracles and prophecies . . . Others deny the historical value and nature of the documents of revelation almost a priori. (Part 2, Sect. V)

The Biblical Commision does have a point.

Differences between NT scholars regarding the gospels often seem unbridgeable and most seem unwilling to accept the degree to which they have been influenced by their own presuppositions. The whole idea of evidence and of a neutral assessment of the position seems to have become impossible. For many biblical scholars God is an irrelevant hypothesis or, at best, a word that is found in the text and whose origins and literary usages can be examined. They consider that it is possible to study the Bible as literature without recourse to consideration of the existence or non-existence of God. It is easy to find, as one example, scholars who will look on the Bible from the perspective of 'radical feminism' and this then colours their whole understanding and approach. This is not to say that radical feminism is right or wrong – just that it is a prior position that is being brought to bear on the texts. Attaining neutrality is exceptionally difficult but at the least biblical scholars should be able to acknowledge their own presuppositions and how this affects their enquiry.

If there is no God, then it is necessary to evaluate the remainder of the gospel story in different ways. Some scholars may then see Jesus as essentially similar to Sherlock Holmes: as a medium through whom ideas can be expressed which may still be relevant and true. For instance, just as it may be possible to hold that the Sherlock Holmes stories are 'true' because they express fundamental insights into the nature of good detective work, so the Jesus story may be held to be 'true' in that it shows human beings something about how life should be lived and about the importance of love, compassion, forgiveness and care of neighbour which is valid for all human beings in all circumstances. One could talk of knowing 'the mind of Sherlock Holmes' or 'the mind of Jesus' and there would be a broad equivalence between these two claims.

A number of philosophers take this latter approach. They maintain that Christianity is 'true' in that it enshrines, embodies and preserves these human insights and that the Christian story provides a way of communicating these values to subsequent generations. What is really important is the *spirit* of Jesus' message, not the historical Jesus: that love not Law should rule; that seeking power, money and reputation are the wrong aims in life; that all human beings are equal regardless of race or background. To be sure, they add, other stories might achieve the same result. For instance, the story of the Buddha might be held to preserve similar insights.

This approach is taken by Don Cupitt. In *What is a Story?* he maintains that the Christian story is essentially fictitious but preserves insights by which he and others choose to live. Professor R. Coote of San Francisco Theological Seminary and the Revd D.R. Ord, writing in a book called *Is the Bible True?* (SCM, 1994), put their position like this:

> Many biblical stories are like *Animal Farm*. They are true, although not historically accurate or factual. They are concerned with proclaiming a message, not with providing us with a chronology of events from the history of Israel or the life of Jesus of Nazareth. We must learn to read them not as history but as message. (p. 33)

Modern revisionary accounts of Christianity which dispense with God follow in a long tradition which interprets the gospel story entirely in human terms.

Von Buren was a prominent theologian but, philosophically, he was essentially a verificationist. Verificationists maintain that in order to be meaningful a statement has to be capable of verification. Clearly the story of the resurrection cannot be verified therefore it would, if one is a verificationist, not be meaningful. Von Buren therefore gave an account of the gospel story that could be understood entirely without God. As he says:

> The man who says 'Jesus is Lord' is saying that the history of Jesus . . . has exercised a liberating effect on him, and that he has been so grasped by it that it has become the historical norm of his perspective on life. (*The Secular Meaning of the Gospel,* 1963, p. 141)

For Von Buren, Christian faith is liberating and it is 'catching', indeed he actually uses the word 'contagion'. People are grasped by the effects of the story of Jesus. They find in relating themselves to this story and living by it they become free, and their example leads to others choosing to live by the story as well. God is irrelevant in this view – as irrelevant at the time of the events the gospel stories are meant to describe as today. Sherlock Holmes and Jesus are, essentially, similar.

Von Buren, Coote, Ord and Cupitt, in their different ways, are examples of people who have been deeply affected by the impact of the story of the gospels, particularly the challenging ethical demand they make upon all human beings. For them, the divinity of Jesus is irrelevant to this story and therefore they interpret the story according to their own presuppositions. This is a perfectly reasonable approach *provided*, that is, that one shares their opening presuppositions, which include the view that there is no God as traditionally defined.

However approaches such as this reinterpret what is meant by a story being true. If there is no God and if the gospel stories only keep alive a particular way in which human beings can look at the world, then the gospel stories are essentially false. It does not appear that the gospel writers themselves thought in these terms. They were not simply telling stories; they claimed to be 'witnesses' and were making *factual* claims. Of course, these claims may be mistaken, but in that case the claims should be rejected.

The existence of God is, therefore, a presupposition which will vitally affect any claim to the gospel story being true. This presupposition can be framed as follows:

> God exists and is the creator and sustainer of the whole cosmos.
> The people of Israel were God's chosen people and the OT
> provides a record of God's interaction with these people.

Jesus' role

If God exists, then the next issue is to decide on Jesus' relationship
to God. Was he a deluded individual? A rabbi or a prophet? Or was
he something more?

The gospel story is at pains to point out that Jesus stood in a
unique relationship with God. It does this in various ways. It draws
comparisons with Moses and Elijah, the great teacher and the great
prophet respectively of the Jewish tradition. In both cases, however,
it makes clear that Jesus is greater than Moses or Elijah. It also talks
of Jesus as the 'Son of God'.The gospel writers use a variety of
stories to point out Jesus' unique status. John's baptism of Jesus in
the river Jordan – at which the heavens are portrayed as opening and
a dove descending, and in which God is described as saying 'This is
my beloved Son' – is an explicit reference to this status. Jesus' birth
and the extraordinary events attached to it, as well as the symbolism
of these events, is another way in which the evangelists emphasized
Jesus' unique position.

There is no way of establishing that Jesus was in a unique relationship with God. Each reader of the gospels has to make a decision
about this for her or himself. The lack of 'proof' for Jesus' unique
relationship to God is acknowledged by the evangelists. When John
the Baptist's disciples come to Jesus asking:

> Are you the one who is to come, or are we to wait for another?
> (Luke 7:20)

Jesus is not recorded as replying, 'Yes, I am the one!' Instead John's
disciples are told to go back to the prison where John is held and to
report what they have seen – John must make up his own mind.

The same ambiguity occurs when Jesus asks his followers:

Who do the crowds say that I am? (Luke 9:18)

His followers say that some people say he is John the Baptist come back from the dead, others that he is Elijah or one of the prophets. Jesus then asks the disciples:

But who do you say that I am? (Luke 9:20)

The disciples are presented with a choice and it is Peter who gives the reply: 'The Messiah of God.' Peter is affirming the truth of Jesus' uniqueness, but no proof is possible. The gospels set out the alternatives and the reader must decide.

No amount of biblical research or theological study will be able to validate these claims. Theology may examine the consequences of making these statements, but it *cannot show the statements to be true*. To talk, therefore, of the truth of this statement is to express a personal faith commitment, it is to stand for a particular position.

It must be emphasized that lack of evidence does *not* mean the same as falsity. To take this position is to adopt a 'verificationist' approach to truth – in other words, to maintain that a statement cannot be held to be true unless it can be verified. Verificationists are on weak philosophic ground. It may not be possible to prove that there is intelligent life on a planet in a galaxy far removed from ours which we may never be able to reach, but it is nevertheless perfectly reasonable to hold that *either* there is *or* there is not such life. Similarly, lack of evidence for Jesus being God does not rule out the claim that *either* he was *or* he was not.

The second claim of the gospel story is, therefore:

Jesus stands in a unique relationship with God.

He transcends Moses or Elijah and he represents God to human beings in a way in which no other person has ever done.

Summary

Stage One of the gospel story involves two claims:

- God exists and is the creator and sustainer of the whole cosmos. The people of Israel were God's chosen people and the OT provides a record of God's interaction with these people.
- Jesus stands in a unique relationship with God.

NINETEEN

Resurrection

Stage two

Imagine that you lived in Palestine soon after Jesus was born or that you were a Jew living in one of the cities of the Roman Empire. Stories might reach you about Jesus. At first you would have no difficulty in identifying with these stories. You would probably see Jesus as Elijah or Moses, or a new Elijah or Moses. However, as you heard more, you would quickly see that a bigger claim than that was being made. Your interest about this man might be excited and you might want to meet him, but you would then learn that he was dead. Not only was he dead, he died as a criminal, crucified by the Romans. This would have been much harder to accept. Elijah did not die at all; he entered God's kingdom directly through God's intervention. Yet this new, 'greater than Elijah' was killed by Israel's enemies in a way that indicated that he was an outcast, a nobody. You would then be told that not only did he die, he also rose from the dead. This you would probably find very difficult to believe. This was not a traditional Jewish image and you would probably find it implausible. Nevertheless this was the claim that was being made.

The resurrection is the key to the gospel story. It is the truth of the claim to Jesus' resurrection that is rejected by so many scholars. Once this is rejected then Jesus becomes just another human being – perhaps a remarkable human being with profound insights into how life should be lived, but another human being nevertheless. If the existence of God is the key initial presupposition for the validity of the gospel story then the coping stone of the whole story must be whether or not Jesus actually rose from the dead.

It is not entirely clear what it means to rise from the dead, although the gospel stories give remarkably consistent accounts. Jesus was embodied, his body had disappeared from the tomb. He ate with his disciples and they could see the marks of the nails and the spear mark in his side. He did not rise as a 'soul' or spirit, which might have been the expected outcome if Greek philosophic thought determined the way the story was written. Greek thought tended to be dualist and those who believed in life after death (such as Socrates, Plato and their later followers) considered that it was the disembodied soul that survived. This led to a somewhat negative view of the body in Greek thought. This idea influenced later Christian thinkers who tended to downgrade anything physical and to see the body as the prison house of the soul. However this is not a biblical idea. The Hebrews thought of the human being as a unity, not as a body and soul, and the resurrection of the whole person would have been much more in accordance with Jewish thinking than with Greek.

Jews did not always believe in the resurrection of the dead and the gospel texts make clear that there was an ongoing debate within Judaism at the time of Jesus (cf. Luke 20:27-39). Some did not believe in any resurrection, whilst others did. Belief in the resurrection arose after the rebellion led by Judas Maccabbaeus (the 'Hammer of the Gentiles') against the Seleucid forces of occupation in *c.* 170 BC when tens of thousands of Jews died. It has been suggested that this belief was influenced by a Zoroastrian idea but it coincided with a felt need to provide some hope, given the huge scale of the deaths in the rebellion.

Muslims revere Jesus as a prophet and consider that he was conceived virginally. They have a devotion to Mary and endorse the gospels, except in so far as they conflict with the Koran. However they do not consider that Jesus died on the cross, rather they maintain that he was taken down while still alive. On this basis, the story of the crucifixion and resurrection would be false. In comparison, some Jews acknowledge Jesus as a rabbi, but certainly reject any claim to divine status or to his having been resurrected. There is no final proof of the resurrection and, again, readers of the gospels are left to make up their own minds. However there may be indicators as to the truth or falsity of the story.

Possibly the best pointer to the accuracy of the reports of the resurrection is the conduct of Jesus' followers after his death. Given that their leader had been killed one would have expected them to go into hiding and to return to their normal jobs. The Acts of the Apostles portrays them fearing the Jewish authorities, and individuals like Saul were set on eliminating Jesus' followers. Stephen was stoned to death by an angry crowd not long after Jesus' death (Acts 7). However the reaction of Jesus' followers was exactly the opposite of what everyone expected. After the initial few days, before the resurrection, they behaved as one might expect – keeping a very low profile indeed. Soon after the resurrection, however, they spoke out with total confidence and vigour and were not even frightened of death. They rejoiced after their master's death and were totally certain that he had risen from the dead. With incredible rapidity their story spread throughout the Roman world and further afield. Those who reject the resurrection need to account for this transformation in the conduct of Jesus' followers. It may be argued that the simplest explanation is that the events happened as described.

The extraordinary claim that Jesus should be indentified with God came as a direct result of the experience of the risen Jesus. It may be argued that it was not the faith of the early Christians which gave rise to the belief that Jesus rose from the dead, rather it was the conviction that Jesus rose from the dead which gave rise to the faith of the early Christians.

As C.F.D. Moule says:

The only really distinctive thing for which Christians stood was their declaration that Jesus had been raised from the dead according to God's design and the consequent estimate of him as in a unique sense Son of God and representative of man . . . (*The Phenomenon of the New Testament*, p. 18)

W. Pannenberg (*Jesus – God and Man*, SCM, 1978) argues along similar lines:

> The Easter appearances are not to be explained from the Easter faith of the disciples; rather, conversely, the Easter faith is to be explained from the appearances. (p. 88)

However, although Pannenberg is convinced that the resurrection happened broadly as the gospel story describes, this leads to his being far more sceptical about the historical truth of the remainder of the gospel material. His argument is that the disciples would have been so overwhelmed by the fact of the resurrection that the historical details of Jesus' life would have mattered very little and may have been largely the result of myth-making by the early Christian writers.

There is a problem here, not only in balancing probabilities but also in trying to determine the motives of the early gospel writers. Some commentators work under the implicit assumption that the evangelists' ideas of truth and falsity were radically different from those of today. But there seems little evidence for this. If the resurrection did, indeed, occur, then it seems more likely that the disciples would have tried as hard as possible to record the details of the events leading up to that resurrection. Certainly there may have been differences of perspective or of recollection – one would expect that of human beings recording any story. However such minor differences are close to what is found in the gospels and there seems little clear basis for widespread scepticism.

If, therefore, we had lived in the first century AD and heard of the story of Jesus, we would have had to make a decision about the accuracy or otherwise of his reported resurrection. Initial incredulity would probably have been our reaction, but many people claimed to have seen the risen Jesus and we would have had to balance the evidence. The gospels claim that the story of the resurrection is true and the rapid spread of Christianity indicates that many contemporaries quickly accepted this claim.

The gospel story, however, moves beyond the claim that Jesus rose from the dead. It also claims that Jesus ascended into heaven. This idea would have been more familiar to Jews than the resurrection as they would have been well aware of the story of Elijah. The gospels go on to assert that *all* human beings will rise from the dead. A universal claim is therefore being made. As we have seen, there were Jewish groups who would have identified with this claim and so this would have been picking up a theme already present in Jewish society. What is more, the story claims that all human beings will be judged after death and that what will happen to them will depend on how they have lived. The evangelists make this point in many of the stories about Jesus, Such as the parables of the farmer and his barns (Luke 12:13–21), the narrow door (Luke 13:22–30) or the weeds (Matthew 13:24–30).

The gospel story, therefore, is not just about a claimed historical event – it is about a historical event that has decisive significance for the person who listens to it. It challenges the individual and forces a decision, a decision about its truth or falsity.

Summary

The second stage of the gospel story can, therefore, be expressed as follows:

• Jesus rose from the dead as an individual and appeared in bodily form to his friends and to other followers. When he finally left them he promised to come again. All human beings will survive death as individuals and will be judged on the basis of their lives on earth.

TWENTY

The Significance of Jesus

The central part of the gospel story about Jesus has now been set out. Those who listened to the early followers of Jesus would either have accepted or rejected the story of the resurrection at this stage. If they found it too incredible to be true, then they would have listened no further. If, however, they accepted it, then it would become necessary to tell them more about Jesus – about his life and why God allowed him to die; about why death was a victory and not a defeat; about what he had taught; and about his significance to those who followed him. The description of Jesus' life and ministry should, therefore, be seen as effectively 'unpacking' the resurrection story. In a way, the resurrection story came first from the listeners' point of view, and their attitude to that story would determine their attitude to the rest of the material. The next stage, then, is to talk about Jesus' early life.

Stage three

Jesus' birth

The gospel writers wish to point out Jesus' significance yet not all of them do this in the same way. Mark starts with Jesus' ministry, John with the pre-existent Word of God, and Matthew and Luke tell stories of Jesus' birth.

Matthew and Luke are effectively telling their readers that even at Jesus' birth his significance can be seen. Their stories show God's action in the conception and birth of Jesus and again point to his unique status. The humble birthplace of the new king emphasizes that God's ways are not the world's ways – God constantly surprises and works in ways that are unexpected. The themes of shepherds and wise men point to the 'outsiders' who recognize Jesus for who he is and are contrasted with Herod's plotting. The 'insider'/ 'outsider' distinction is at work at this early stage. At the birth God's hand is present: God is portrayed as guiding events by thwarting the plans of those who oppose him (symbolized by Herod) and protecting Jesus from harm by sending him to Egypt.

It is important for Matthew, in particular, to show Jesus' descent from David through Joseph. Yet, at the same time, Matthew and Luke are saying that Jesus is God's Son. It appears that there is a contradiction here: either Jesus was conceived without Mary making love to Joseph (or anyone else), in which case Jesus is not descended from David; or Jesus was Joseph's natural son, in which case Jesus was not conceived by divine agency. If one wanted to continue to maintain that he was the unique 'Son of God', one would have to accept an 'adoptionist' position whereby Jesus was a normal human being who was effectively 'adopted' by God at the time of his baptism by John.

However this is to miss what is taking place in the story. The gospel writers are trying to say two things: firstly, that Jesus is uniquely related to God and secondly, that he is a descendant of David and therefore the one to whom God's promises to David point. Theological points are being made by means of a story. The theological points may be valid and true even though a story-form is being used to convey them. To regard these stories as literal accounts is to misunderstand their significance. They are means used by the evangelists for explaining the significance of Jesus to their readers and to those to whom the gospel message is preached. This does not mean, however, that there are no literal truth claims underlying the gospel story. There may be, but this is not of central importance.

Only Matthew records the story of the wise men. It is worth noting that there is no reference in the gospels to there being three of them. This is a story that has been built up over the years possibly because there is a reference to three gifts (2:11). (See p. 24 for an explanation of the wise men's theological significance.) Also, only Matthew records Herod's killing all the children, aged two years and under, in Bethlehem (2:16). At first sight this may seem an incredible story, but in a century which has witnessed Auschwitz, Stalin's death camps, the murderous killings of the Pol Pot regime in Cambodia or the slaughter in Rwanda, the killing of children by Herod to preserve his dynasty can seem positively plausible. It is not, however, the literal details that are decisive for the gospel writers, it is their theological significance.

There are some apparent contradictions between the texts which are not material to the gospel writers. For instance, Matthew says that 'Jesus was born in Bethlehem of Judea' (2:1). After going to Egypt:

> . . . he made his home in a town called Nazareth, so that what had been spoken through the prophets might be fulfilled, 'He will be called a Nazarean.' (Matthew 2:23)

Thus Mary and Joseph are portrayed as not having lived in Nazareth but only going to the city to fulfil a prophecy. They would have gone to Judea if they had felt the danger from Herod. This picture is radically different from that given in Luke, who has them coming from Nazareth all along. After Luke's birth story, complete with shepherds and angels, Jesus goes to Jerusalem to be presented in the Temple. Luke has no mention of Herod or the flight to Egypt. Then:

> When they had finished doing everything required by the Law of the Lord [in Jerusalem] they returned to Galilee, to their own town of Nazareth. (Luke 2:39)

In other words, Luke paints a picture of a peaceful childhood and a return to the family's long-term home in Nazareth. Again, we cannot be sure of the precise details but it is not the details that are important.

Once the resurrection has been accepted, then it is the theological significance of Jesus' birth and childhood that is decisive. Readers of the gospels in Jesus' time would have recognized this. It may be that the modern reader, who is reluctant to see the significance lying beneath the story-form, misses the real understanding of what is being done. This is one reason why source and form criticism may be such flawed methods of biblical analysis. They break the story into pieces and lose the reality that the whole expresses. As an example, imagine an old and slightly deranged man picking flowers and pulling them apart. He names every part – petal, sepal, carpel, anther, etc. – however he destroys the reality of the flower as he cannot 'see' the totality. Some biblical scholars are like this old man.

John the Baptist

John the Baptist is a herald. He proclaims the 'one who is to come' and he can be seen as having the role that Elijah was prophesied to have in proclaiming the coming of the Messiah. John the Baptist is a central figure in all the gospel accounts and he provides another occasion for Jesus' significance to be disclosed. The story of John also provides the gospel writer with an opportunity to emphasize the important theme of a call to repentance and baptism.

It is significant that John the Baptist was portrayed as preaching in the wilderness. The wilderness was not just a place but it was also a powerful symbol. John was not preaching in the Temple, instead by staying in the wilderness his opposition to the current structures within Israel is symbolized. More than this, it was in the wilderness that the people of Israel had wandered after leaving slavery in Egypt. It was also from the wilderness that God's prophets often called to the people (cf. Isaiah 40:3).

John the Baptist's relation to Jesus is not clear, and the Synoptic gospels and John give different accounts. Mark's gospel says:

. . . Jesus came from Nazareth of Galilee and was baptized by John in the Jordan. And just as he was coming up out of the water, he saw the heavens torn apart . . . And the Spirit immediately drove him out into the wilderness. (1:9-12)

In other words, Mark's gospel has Jesus being baptized right at the beginning. Also, in the three Synoptics John's arrest is the moment that Jesus starts his own ministry (Mark 1:14).

John's gospel gives a totally different picture. In fact the evangelist can be seen as picturing John and Jesus preaching baptism and repentance from sin at the same time, although not together. John does not baptize Jesus, although he is very specific that Jesus 'ranks ahead of me' (1:30) and is 'the Son of God' (1:34). John's disciples complained that many people were going to Jesus and not to John:

> [John's disciples] came to John and said to him, 'Rabbi, the one who was with you across the Jordan, to whom you testified, here he is baptizing, and all are going to him!' (3:26)

It may be that John the evangelist records this earlier ministry of Jesus while the Synoptics do not. Thus the one source may amplify the others. It may also be that the evangelist has attributed words to John the Baptist which reflected the later Church's understanding of Jesus. John and Jesus were not, however, preaching competing messages. There was unanimity between them on the need for repentance and baptism. What is more, concentration on these details of the story misses the theological point, which depends on John's role as proclaimer, as herald to Jesus. This, for the evangelists, is the truly significant point and the chronology is unimportant.

John the Baptist and Jesus were both 'outsiders', obedient to God but rejecting the norms of the society in which they lived (Matthew 11:7–10, 16–19; Luke 7:24–7, 31–5). The other side of the sinfulness of all human beings was Jesus' promise of salvation for people from all walks of life, no matter what their rank or position. The only requirement was for the individual to acknowledge her or his own need and failure. This was a very important message in the early years of Christianity. The early Christians were proclaiming a universal message and, more particularly, were breaking down the old barriers so that God's promise and salvation were on offer to the most marginalized of peoples.

The prophets in the OT felt that they had been called by God to speak to his people. Jesus' baptism by John also functions in this way. Jesus has a vision of the heavens opening and a voice saying that he is God's Son. Jesus is recorded as being convinced that he was sent from God (e.g. Matthew 5:17; 10:34–6; 11:19; 15:24; Mark 1:38; 2:17; 10:45; Luke 7:34, 10:16; 12:49). Some of these passages may, of course, have been attributed to Jesus by his followers, but they certainly represented an early conviction shared by the first Christians of how Jesus saw his role. It is significant that whilst OT prophets introduced their prophecy with 'Thus says the Lord', Jesus is recorded as saying 'I say to you'. Jesus is portrayed as claiming a distinct authority of his own, although all the sayings which appear to confer this authority are confined to Matthew 5. Of course, this may increase the possibility that they are due to the editor.

One argument employed against Jesus being seen as the Messiah (by those who heard about him but rejected his claims) was that the prophet Malachi had said that before the Messiah came, Elijah would first come (Malachi 4:5). Jesus' answer was simple: Elijah had already come in the form of John the Baptist.

> Then they asked him, 'Why do the scribes say that Elijah must come first?' He said to them, . . . 'I tell you that Elijah has come and they did to him whatever they pleased . . .' (Mark 9:11–13)

This, of course, means that John the Baptist's death can also be seen as a pointer to the suffering of the Messiah, since Isaiah 53:3–7 indicates:

> He was despised and rejected by others; a man of suffering and acquainted with infirmity . . . he was wounded for our transgressions, crushed for our iniquities . . . All we like sheep have gone astray; we have all turned to our own way, and the Lord has laid

on him the iniquity of us all . . . like a lamb that is led to the slaughter, and like a sheep that before its shearers is silent, so he did not open his mouth.

This 'suffering servant' imagery would have been very familiar to first-century Jews and the gospel writers identify Jesus with this image.

It seems entirely possible that John the Baptist did preach as the gospels indicate, however his indentification with Elijah seems much more debatable and may have been added by the gospel writers to ensure that a particular OT prophecy was seen as being fulfilled. It may well have been that John baptized Jesus, although it is possible that this theme could have been imposed later as a way of reconciling disciples of Jesus and John. Certainly Jesus may have had a vision at his baptism and this may have been of great significance for him, but whether this is attributed to God or not will depend to a large degree on whether the reader has accepted the initial presuppositions about God's existence and Jesus' unique status.

Summary

Stage Three of the gospel story can be summarized as follows:

• Jesus' birth and early childhood show his special relationship to God and God's providential care for him. They also show how Jesus fulfils the OT prophecies about the Messiah.
• John's baptizing activity, in a wilderness area south of Jerusalem using water from the river Jordan, points forward to the coming of Jesus as Messiah. John is a herald emphasizing the need for everyone to repent and turn to God and preparing people for the advent of Jesus and his message.

TWENTY-ONE

Jesus' Life and Message

The first three stages of the gospel story are by far the most important. If the truth of these are accepted, then the remaining stages expound the significance of Jesus. Once someone has accepted Jesus' status as coming from God, and his significance as being God's unique messenger, then it would obviously be important for them to learn about his life and teachings, and within them the message he wished to convey and how people could follow him. The gospel writers make this clear by describing Jesus' life.

Stage Four

Jesus' life and message

In the wilderness Jesus is depicted as being tempted by the Devil. He is described as rejecting the possibility of using his power to convince people to follow him; he rejects the possibility of just catering to his own and other people's physical needs by providing food; and he rejects making his identity explicit. This was a radical approach because it showed the power of God as lying in weakness rather than cosmic strength. The world is in the power of forces of darkness rather than God, although the gospel writers make clear that, in the final analysis, this power is illusory and will be overcome by the power of God. The likelihood is high that this view of God's power expresses a truth that Jesus was trying to convey, namely that God's power is 'other than' the world's power.

Jesus is portrayed by the evangelists as seeing himself as having a prophetic and teaching role. At the beginning of Mark's gospel Jesus is recorded 'as one who had authority, and not as the scribes' (1:22). Jesus, like John the Baptist, preached repentance and the forgiveness of sins. He also called individuals to follow him. This was unusual as it was normal in Judaism for pupils to take the initiative in studying under a rabbi. This again points to Jesus' significance: he cannot be seen as just another charismatic rabbi, but is much more than this.

Jesus' call is portrayed as being radical and very uncomfortable. The gospels record him as saying that his followers had to be willing to leave everything to follow him, including their homes, families and jobs. Peter says to Jesus, 'Look, we have left everything and followed you', and Jesus' reply is significant:

> Truly I tell you, there is no one who has left house or brothers or sisters or mother or father or children or fields, for my sake and for the sake of the good news, who will not receive a hundredfold . . . (Mark 10:28–30)

Mark 3:31–5 gives the same message: Jesus is portrayed as being indifferent to his earthly family – not just as pointing to a post-resurrection state but also to the 'new family' formed by his followers. One of Jesus' most radical sayings comes in response to someone who wishes to follow him but who first asks to be allowed to go and bury his father. Jesus replies:

> Let the dead bury their dead, but as for you, go and proclaim the kingdom of God. (Luke 9:60)

Graham Stanton suggests that 'the dead' are the spiritually dead who can carry out the customary Jewish burial rites, but Jesus' followers have a higher priority. Loyalty and obedience to God go before everything else.

Love is also at the centre of Jesus' message – *non-preferential love* which reaches out beyond the normal boundaries of family, tribe and society to embrace all human beings. Jesus broke down all the traditional barriers; all human beings were to be seen as God's children.

All the Synoptic gospel writers say that Jesus preached the coming of 'the kingdom of God', although Matthew tends to use the term 'the kingdom of heaven' – probably to follow the Jewish practice of avoiding the use of the word 'God'. Jews recognized God's unique, sovereign status and were well aware of the danger of making him into something like a 'superman' figure. They also approached God with an awe which is rare today. By contrast to Matthew's use of the 'kingdom of heaven', John's gospel only has two references to 'the kingdom' (John 3:5; 18:36). The kingdom of God almost certainly related to OT teachings which saw God as king. The kingdom of God is to be found where God's commands rule, either in this world or in a world to come after the Last Judgement.

The miracle stories belong to the oldest part of the gospel tradition. The gospels themselves say that Jesus was not the only one who performed miracles (e.g. Luke 11:19) and the early Christians valued these stories as 'signs' of Jesus' position. The gospel writers appear to have been restrained in attributing miracles to Jesus. Many more dramatic miracles could have been conceived if this was the intention of the writers and, as we have seen, in some of the early stories about Jesus circulating in other texts more unlikely miracles were performed (cf. p. 106). The miracles recorded in the gospels mostly point to fulfilment of prophecy. Thus Isaiah says:

> Then the eyes of the blind shall be opened, and the ears of the deaf unstopped; then the lame shall leap like a deer, and the tongue of the speechless sing for joy. (35:5–6)

Even the gospel writers did not think the miracles would prove Jesus' status – they were pointers, but the truth would only be seen by those ready to acknowledge it (Mark 4:11; 8:18).

Attitudes to the truth of the miracles stories will depend on whether one accepts previous statements, including God's existence and Jesus' unique relationship with God. If these are accepted, then the miracles are not particularly problematic, although the interests of the gospel writers in attributing miracles to Jesus which confirm his status would need to be recognized. If the existence of God is rejected, then the miracle stories will be as well.

The Synoptic gospels all record Jesus using parables frequently (cf. Chapter 14), yet John's gospel never uses the word 'parable' at all. The individual gospel writers use the parables in different places and sometimes they add their own introductions and endings, in the latter case explaining the meaning of the story. As we have seen in Mark's gospel, Jesus is depicted as explaining the parables privately to his disciples. Matthew expands Mark's chapter on parables (Mark 4) in his chapter 13. There seems little doubt that Jesus himself used parables, although it is impossible to be sure which of the parables or parts of the individual parable stories should be attributed to Jesus himself and which have been added by the gospel writers. Again, this is not the vital point and would not have been the prime concern of the gospel writers. They were trying to communicate the message and the call of their risen Lord and they used the stories told about him to explain the nature of the call. The issue is not 'Were the details precisely as recorded?' but 'Do the stories accurately reflect the message that Jesus wished to convey?'

Jesus' life can be summarized in various ways, but one possibility might be:

> Jesus was tempted to pursue a different lifestyle but chose obedience to God. He gathered together a group of disciples and preached forgiveness of sins, the need to respond to God in loving obedience, and the coming of the kingdom of God. He broke down the barriers between 'insider' and 'outsider' and showed, through his life, that God called every human being to follow him. He used parables to communicate his message and performed miraculous signs.

Faith or offence

A highly significant theme which occurs throughout the gospels yet which modern translations frequently obscure is the choice between 'faith' and 'offence'. The words 'offence' or 'scandal' hardly appear in modern translations, but in the Greek version 'offence' is extremely common. The Greek word for 'offence' or 'scandal' is *skandalon*. Wherever this appears in the biblical text it is:

. . . translated in the RSV as 'cause for stumbling', 'cause of sin', 'difficulty', 'hindrance', 'hindrance in the way', 'make fall', 'pitfall', 'stumbling block', 'tempation' or 'temptation to sin'. (McCracken, *The Scandal of the Gospels*, OUP, 1994, p. 8)

The same translation problem occurs in most other modern versions so it is not surprising that the *scandal* and *offence* of Jesus is no longer portrayed. Yet it is central to the gospel story.

Many of Jesus' sayings are scandalous: he calls people to follow him and to put their families in second place; to renounce their wealth; to give up everything for the sake of the kingdom; to give away their coats; to give no thought for tomorrow; to trust God totally and to have faith in him rather than in themselves. It is, indeed, an offensive message, and in Jesus' time, just as today, people would prefer not to be 'offended'. They would prefer either to make Jesus' message 'acceptable' or else to transform Jesus into a purely human, non-radical figure.

Confronted by the figure of Jesus, two reactions are possible. The one will involve rejecting him and the other will involve accepting him and his message, in faith. The offence/faith decision is a crucial one for every human being. Rationally, the choice of 'offence' may well seem the more plausible. After all, how can a man be God? How can a creature be the creator? It would be much more reasonable to claim, as many biblical scholars do, that Jesus was an ordinary man and must be understood in his cultural setting.

Many modern accounts of Jesus stem from trying to see him in terms of his cultural setting and speculating on how he would have been seen by his contemporaries. These accounts do not start from the gospels themselves – they all start with an assumption which identifies Jesus with a particular type of person or a specific figure, and then interpret the gospels in this light. Everything depends, therefore, on this initial identification. All these accounts involve taking 'offence' against the idea that Jesus was sent from God, was in a unique relationship with God and, indeed, was God. The accounts are perfectly plausible; indeed they may be *more* plausible than the traditional Christian claim. The accounts of Jesus' teachings showed that he expected nothing less.

The distinction between '*faith*' and '*offence*' was specifically recognized by Soren Kierkegaard in his book *Philosophic Fragments*, but attention has been drawn to it recently by David McCracken in *The Scandal of the Gospels* (OUP, 1994). There are many places where this theme occurs but Matthew 15 is a good example. The Pharisees came to Jesus complaining that his disciples did not wash before they ate. Jesus points out that is is the Pharisees who try to make fools of God – they obey their own rules rather than God's commands, and Jesus insults them:

> You hypocrites! How right Isaiah was when he prophesied about you! 'These people, says God, honour me with their words but their heart is really far away from me.' (Matthew 15:7–8 NEB)

Jesus' disciples come to him and say, 'Do you know that the Pharisees were offended by you?' (15:12). It is not surprising they were offended. However the NEB blunts this language and substitutes: 'Did you know that the Pharisees had their feelings hurt?' – which rather lacks the punch of 'offended'. Jesus explains to the disciples that the Pharisees have taken offence because they are blind to his message, and have chosen to be blind. They have fallen into the pit because of their blindness, which is due to their having taken offence at him; they would not recognize him for who he was. Jesus even gets angry with his disciples for their failure to understand. He is not portrayed as a patient man.

The next part of Matthew 15 makes the position even clearer. Jesus went to an area near Tyre and Sidon and a Canaanite woman came to him asking him to help her possessed daughter. Jesus is thoroughly rude to her: he says she is not an Israelite; she is a dog. (Imagine calling a woman today, a mother of a sick child, a bitch!) One would expect her to be offended, but she is not. As McCracken puts it:

> More astonishing than the insult is the woman's response. She, unlike the Pharisees, affirms the insult ('Yes, Lord') choosing not to be offended. She has acknowledged his lordship and his Jewishness from the outset ('Lord, Son of David'). Even in the face of an insult that would normally send one away from the giver of the insult enraged or in despair, she continues to acknowledge his lordship and is therefore willing to accept the role of dog. She, like the dogs, will willingly take the crumbs, for these crumbs, she believes, are life-giving bread from the Lord, and they will heal her daughter. Jesus' response – 'Woman, great is your faith' – is in direct contrast to his response to Peter in the preceding chapter when Peter began to sink in the water ('You of little faith, why did you doubt?' Matthew 14:31) and to all the disciples in the following chapter ('You of little faith . . . Do you still not perceive?' Matthew 16:8–9). (The *Scandal of the Gospels*, pp. 18–19)

Jesus is constantly *unreasonable*. He calls his followers to forgive people not seventy times but seventy times seven. He says that a child is the greatest in the kingdom of heaven. Imagine the reaction to this if you were a devout or 'holy' man or woman who spent your life keeping the religious rules. Jesus is 'at home' with the outcasts, those who are rejected by 'respectable' society. A despised Samaritan is the 'good neighbour'. His disciples are told that they have to eat and drink his flesh and blood, at which they nearly took offence saying, 'This teaching is difficult. Who can accept it?' (John 6:60). Their reaction was not surprising as it is difficult to think of anything more offensive that Jesus could have said. It breached Jewish taboos against cannibalism and even the strong prohibition against the drinking of blood.

Faith is found where it is least expected: in the hated tax collector who leaves everything to follow Jesus; in the Roman centurion who trusts Jesus so much that he does not even want him to come to his house; in the adulterer's tears; or in the words of the penitent thief on the cross.

Part of the problem with the idea of offence is that today Jesus is portrayed as 'gentle Jesus meek and mild', the kind and loving hero. He was nothing of the sort. His message was radical and challenging and it would offend most people; it shattered their complacency and disrupted the status quo. Norman Perrin (*Jesus and the Language of the Kingdom: Symbol and Metaphor in New Testament Interpretation*, Fortress Press, 1976) has referred to the 'process of domestication' of parables and other stories, so much so that people today do not even notice the offence that they portray. The gospels have been sanitized and, in the process, their meaning may have been destroyed.

Summary

The position as portrayed in the gospels with regard to Jesus' message and the faith/offence distinction (Stage Four) can be summarized as follows:

• Jesus was tempted to pursue a different lifestyle but chose obedience to God. He gathered together a group of disciples and preached forgiveness of sins, the need to respond to God in loving obedience, and the coming of the kingdom of God. He broke down the barriers between 'insider' and 'outsider' and showed, through his life, that God called every human being to follow him. He used parables to communicate his message and performed miraculous signs.

• Jesus stands opposed to the present worldly order which rejects him and tries to suppress his message, which is also God's message. He presents people with a choice – either faith or offence.

TWENTY-TWO

The Last Week

Jesus is portrayed by the gospel writers as setting out for Jerusalem, eating a meal with his disciples, being arrested, and then being tried and crucified. The details vary significantly between the Synoptics and John, but they all present this essential structure. The final stage takes us back to Stage Three and shows that Jesus' death was not the disaster it appeared to be: it should be seen as a victory, not a defeat.

Stage Five

Jesus' last meal with his disciples

Jesus' command to remember him in the breaking of bread may either have been accurately recorded by some of the gospel writers or could have been attributed to him to express a meal instituted by the young Christian Church. What seems certain is that the practice of Jesus' followers having a ritual meal together rapidly became accepted within the first Christian communities. This lends support to the view that Jesus did, indeed, give instructions on these lines. It was not an idea that would have been familiar to Jews and the disciples themselves even seemed to have some difficulty with it (John 6:53–60; 1 Corinthians 11 see also p. 218).

Yet if the first three stages of this summary of the gospel story have been accepted, then this event seems highly probable. Even if these stages are not accepted, there seems a high degree of likelihood that this practice goes back to a command from Jesus.

Jesus' crucifixion

The crucifixion of Jesus seems entirely likely. Jesus would have been regarded as a trouble-maker by the Temple authorities, who were concerned to maintain their religious freedoms which had been permitted by the Romans. Jesus would have been seen as a threat, not just against them but against the status quo. We have already seen that Jesus caused offence, he upset people and disrupted the established order. The Temple leaders might well have condemned him and would have had to get Roman approval for the death sentence. Jesus would also have been seen as a threat by the Roman authorities. If, indeed, large crowds flocked to him this would undoubtedly have been reported to them and they might well have seen him as an agitator and the focus of possible rebellion. If Jesus was seen as claiming a 'kingship' role, this could have been construed as a challenge to Caesar and would have attracted immediate Roman attention. However it is impossible to determine whether the Jewish leaders or the Roman authorities were responsible for Jesus' crucifixion.

The evangelists clearly had their own motives for attributing responsibility to one side or the other but it is simply not possible to get back to the actual events. We know from archaeological evidence that crucifixion was used as a form of capital punishment at the time of Jesus. An excavation in Jerusalem in 1968 unearthed a crucified man from the first century AD and one of the Dead Sea Scrolls says that crucifixion was a death reserved for traitors. The trial of Jesus and his crucifixion, therefore, seem entirely probable although the precise details are less clear.

The cosmic significance of Jesus' death

The truth of the claim that Jesus' death and resurrection are events of cosmic significance rests to a very large extent on acceptance of previous claims, including the existence of God, Jesus' unique relationship with God and his fulfilment of the OT prophecies. The cosmic significance of Jesus' death is a theological claim which stems from belief in Jesus and his role and there is no way in which dispassionate enquiry can establish its validity. The gospel writers are at pains to show, however, that the dark forces (to which John refers in his Prologue and to which all the gospel writers refer in the temptations in the wilderness as well as on other occasions) do have a large measure of control in the world. Not all will go well for the forces of light. God's will does not determine that the dark forces cannot inflict pain and suffering on innocent ones.

The problem of innocent suffering perplexed Jewish thinkers since the time the Book of Job was written. This particular text is a genuine attempt to wrestle with the problem. How can there be an omnipotent, wholly good God and yet there be so much evil? (cf. *The Puzzle of Evil* by Peter Vardy). The gospel writers give no answer to that question except that ultimately God triumphs. God's power is shown in weakness. It is in dying that Jesus defeats death; the ultimate power of the world's dark forces is rendered null and void by Jesus' death. Not all, of course, can see this. Many see only Jesus' death, whereas the person of faith also sees the resurrection and, thereby, the defeat of death.

As so often in the gospel story, things are not always what they seem. God and Jesus seem to be defeated on the cross; evil seems to have triumphed. Appearances, however, are deceptive. Death, far from being a defeat, is a victory which leads directly to the foundation and worldwide spread of those who choose to adhere to Jesus and to the God whom they accept he represents.

Summary

The fifth and final stage may be summarized thus:

• Jesus ate with his disciples before he faced trial. He commanded them to remember him in the breaking of bread and the drinking of wine.
• Jesus was condemned to death and was crucified and died on the cross.

• Jesus' crucifixion was an event of cosmic significance. It was the focal point on which history depends. It represented a victory rather than a defeat.

TWENTY-THREE

Bringing the Threads Together

As we have seen, it can be argued that there is a single gospel story held largely in common by the four gospel story writers. It can be summarized as follows:

Stage One
• God exists and is the creator and sustainer of the whole cosmos. The people of Israel were God's chosen people and the OT provides a record of God's interaction with these people.
• Jesus stands in a unique relationship with God.

Stage Two
• Jesus rose from the dead as an individual and appeared in bodily form to his friends and to other followers. When he finally left them he promised to come again. All human beings will survive death as individuals and will be judged on the basis of their lives on earth.

Stage Three
• Jesus' birth and early childhood show his special relationship to God and God's providential care for him. They also show how Jesus fufils the OT prophecies about the Messiah.
• John's baptizing activity in a wilderness area south of Jerusalem using water from the river Jordan, points forward to the coming of Jesus as Messiah. John is a herald emphasizing the need for everyone to repent and turn to God and preparing people for the advent of Jesus and his message.

Stage Four

• Jesus was tempted to pursue a different lifestyle but chose obedience to God. He gathered together a group of disciples and preached forgiveness of sins, the need to respond to God in loving obedience, and the coming of the kingdom of God. He broke down the barriers between 'insider' and 'outsider' and showed, through his life, that God called every human being to follow him. He used parables to communicate his message and performed miraculous signs.

• Jesus stands opposed to the present worldly order which rejects him and tries to suppress his message, which is also God's message. He presents people with a choice – either faith or offence.

Stage Five

• Jesus ate with his disciples before he faced trial. He commanded them to remember him in the breaking of bread and the drinking of wine.

• Jesus was condemned to death and was crucified and died on the cross.

• Jesus' crucifixion was an event of cosmic significance. It was the focal point on which history depends. It represented a victory rather than a defeat.

Parts of this story are, in principle, unverifiable and will depend on individual assessment, particularly whether or not there is a God; whether Jesus stood in a unique relationship to God; and whether Jesus rose from the dead. The question as to whether Jesus' message is faithfully portrayed in the gospel stories is something to which biblical scholarship can certainly contribute, however absolute certainty may be unattainable. Jesus was and remains an ambiguous figure but the gospel accounts fully recognize this.

History or gloss?

Even if the gospel story is held to be true, this will be a matter of an individual's belief or faith, or perhaps the shared conviction of a religious community. No proof is available. Given that religious belief is not tentative, it will represent a commitment which involves a life transformation and a personal decision.

However even if the story is held to be broadly true this should not automatically be extended to cover all the details. As we have seen, the gospel writers may have put their own theological gloss on the events they were describing. Whilst this gloss is important and significant in understanding how the writers, and perhaps their communities, understood Jesus, this is not the same as saying that their accounts accurately represent Jesus' own revelation. The problem arises as to how one separates the gospel writers' theological gloss from the fundamental story and this raises important issues.

There are some statements attributed to Jesus which may or may not have been said by him – there is no way of knowing. What is clear, however, is that any evangelist might have had good reasons for attributing such sayings to Jesus. Examples, and these are no more than examples, include the following:

> I tell you, you are Peter, and on this rock I will build my church, and the gates of Hades will not prevail against it. I will give you the keys of the kingdom of heaven, and whatever you bind on earth will be bound in heaven, and whatever you loose on earth will be loosed in heaven. (Matthew 16:18–19)

The motive for attributing such a statement to Jesus is clear (see p. 184). If Jesus actually said this, then Peter and by implication his successors were given complete power by Jesus. This seems to run counter to much of the rest of Jesus' teaching. Only in one other place does Jesus talk of founding a Church. Indeed, he shows a total lack of awareness of such an institution. There are also passages which seem to indicate that he thought the world would come to an end very soon (cf. Matthew 10:21–3). However evangelists within the Church would have a clear reason for attributing these saying to Jesus as they reinforced the authority of those at the head of the early Church.

> Very truly, I tell you, unless you eat the flesh of the Son of man and drink his blood, you have no life in you. Those who eat my flesh and drink my blood have eternal life, and I will raise them up on the last days. (John 6:53–4)

These, again, are passages that the evangelists might well have had an interest in putting on Jesus' lips as they emphasize that it is only through following Jesus (and therefore taking part in the early Church's rituals) that one can get to God. This exclusivity is in marked contrast to the parable of the sheep and the goats (Matthew 25:31–46) where it is those who feed the hungry and care for prisoners, strangers and the homeless who will get to God's kingdom. All those who ignore the needs of their neighbour will be condemned.

> What God has joined together let no one separate. (Matthew 19:6; cf. Mark 10:9)

This verse appears in Matthew and Mark's gospels. In an infant Church some marriage ceremony would have been performed once it was clear that the end of the world would not come immediately. This ceremony would have been seen as the vehicle for God joining two people together. Divorce would become then, a matter of separating what had been joined together by God. The motive for an evangelist incorporating this verse would be clear, particularly as it may have been seen as representing an extension of Jesus' own teaching.

None of the above examples should be taken to imply that such statements are necessarily glosses on the basic story of Jesus, however they should alert the reader to the possibility. A distinction has to be drawn between the core gospel narrative and possible glosses, and this distinction may have relevance today for people who wish to live by the Christian story.

Attitudes to the Bible differ among Christians. Some maintain that their faith is almost entirely biblically based. Baptists, Calvinists and those in the Reformed Christian tradition tend to rely on this approach. Others see the role of the Church as primary in mediating and transmitting the gospel message. This position tends to be taken by Roman Catholics. Eastern Orthodox, Anglicans and Methodists adopt a middle position, relying heavily on the pronouncements of the early Councils of the Church whilst placing considerably less weight on later Church documents.

The Roman Catholic position tends to be that God has given authority, through Jesus, to the Church. The influence of the Matthean passage quoted above is important here. The coat of arms of the papacy include the 'keys' to the kingdom of heaven held to have been given to Peter and his successors by Jesus in this passage. The Church is inspired by the Holy Spirit thus it can make pronouncements on ethical and other matters secure in the knowledge that these pronouncements are validated by God. Certainly the Catholic Church makes pronouncements on an increasing range of matters for which there is little biblical support (for instance, the prohibition on artificial means of birth control). In recent years the Magisterium of the Catholic Church has moved to increase its influence, requiring those coming forward for ordination as deacons to sign an oath giving 'religious assent of will and intellect to all teachings of the Magisterium' and requiring Catholic teachers in Catholic theological faculties not to teach against the teachings of the Magisterium.

If the Catholic Church has been given authority by God to speak on God's behalf – so that it has been given 'the keys of the kingdom of heaven' and what it 'prohibits on earth will be prohibited in heaven, and what [it] permits on earth will be permitted in heaven' (Matthew 16:18–19) – then there is clear warrant for its claim to authority. If, however, this passage was an addition by the writer of Matthew's gospel, intended to reinforce the position of the fledgling Church's leaders, then it would no longer have the same status.

In the United States, the 'Moral Majority' has become a potent political force, basing its case partly on supposed biblical ethics. The 'Christian Coalition' and the 'New Right' – made up of evangelical Christians and some conservative Catholics – often look to the Bible for certainty in their pronouncements on 'family values' and various moral issues ranging from abortion to homosexuality to genetic engineering. However it is far from clear what 'biblical ethics' are. It may appear easy to quote particular biblical verses to support a position in which one believes, but it should by now be clear that quoting a verse from one of the gospels may not be the same thing as quoting something that Jesus actually said. The quotation may well be the work of an unknown scribe in the first century.

Biblical scholarship can contribute to an increased understanding of such issues and therefore has an important role to play in theological study, however its limits must be recognized. Above all, it may lead to a particular modesty when claiming certainty about what 'Jesus said'. The gospels are a puzzle and those who use them to judge others and to try to ensure adherence to their own positions are unfaithful both to the complexity of the material and to the message attributed to Jesus. The gospels may be valuable for judging ourselves, but they do not provide a framework which can be imposed on others. Jesus never imposed his own views. The call to follow him was always a call – it could be refused.

Jesus wanted to encourage people to take seriously the *spirit* that lay beneath the rules. This spirit can be applied as effectively today as 2,000 years ago. Most of the major moral dilemmas that face people in the present world were not dealt with in the Bible, they were not even considered. Jesus expressed no views on birth control, euthanasia, genetic engineering, surrogate motherhood, abortion in the case of rape, the criterion for a just war, morality in business, environmental ethics or the structural injustices in society. These problems cannot be addressed by selective reading of texts in the gospels. Instead it is necessary to look to the spirit that underlies the gospels, just as Jesus looked to the spirit that lay beneath the Ten Commandments and the Torah. There will be no simple answers – amibiguity and doubt will take the place of simple, unexamined certainties.

The choice between faith and offence remains clear. Even if a faith response is given, then each individual will have to discern how this response should be lived. If the story in the gospels is true, this is how it has to be. The gospel writers wished to engender faith, not by forcing belief but by calling individuals to a free response to the story they had to tell. The call to that free response is still there in the pages of the gospel. Current fashions in biblical criticism may claim that there is no choice to be made; each biblical scholar may loudly claim that he/she has the truth. However most individuals who read the gospels will recognize that it is not as easy as that. Each individual must decide, and then live by that decision. Socrates said:

> I cannot prove the immortality of the soul, but I am ready to stake my life on this 'if'.

Similarly, a modern Christian might say:

> I cannot prove that the gospel story is true, but I stake my life on the claim that it is.

No one can do any more.

Postscript

'Rabbit's clever', said Pooh thoughtfully.
'Yes', said Piglet. 'Rabbit's clever.'
'And he has Brain.'
'Yes', said Piglet, 'Rabbit has Brain.'

There was a long silence.

'I suppose', said Pooh, 'that's why he never understands anything.'

With thanks to A.A. Milne

Selected Further Reading

General

E. Charpentier, *How to Read the New Testament*, SCM, London, 1981.

R.F. Collins, *Introduction to the New Testament*, SCM, London, 1983.

A.M. Hunter, *Introducing the New Testament*, SCM, London, 1972.

W.G. Kümmel, *Introduction to the New Testament*, SCM, London, 1975.

C.J. Roetzel, *The World that Shaped the New Testament*, SCM, London, 1987.

J.B. Bauer (ed.), *Encyclopaedia of Biblical Theology*, Sheed and Ward, London, 1970.

R. Brown, J. Fitzmyer and R. Murphy (eds.), *The New Jerome Biblical Commentary*, Geoffrey Chapman, London, 1990.

Jesus

G. Theissen, *The Shadow of the Galilean*, SCM, London, 1987.

E.P. Sanders, *Jesus and Judaism*, SCM, London, 1984.

G. Vermes, *Jesus and the World of Judaism*, SCM, London, 1983.

N.T. Wright, *Who Was Jesus?*, SPCK, 1992.

Traditions about Jesus

R. Brown, *The Birth of the Messiah*, Doubleday, New York, 1977.

R. Brown, *The Death of the Messiah*, Doubleday, New York, 1994.

G. Ludemann, *The Resurrection of Jesus*, SCM, London, 1994.

G. Stanton, *The Gospels and Jesus*, University Press, Oxford, 1989.

Synoptic Gospels

E.P. Sanders and M. Davies, *Studying the Synoptic Gospels*, SCM, London, 1989.

D.E. Garland, *Reading Matthew*, SPCK, London, 1993.

A. Saldarini, *Matthew's Christian-Jewish Community*, Chicago/London, 1994.

C.E.B. Cranfield, *The Gospel According to St Mark*, University Press, Cambridge, 1989 (reprint).

M. Hengel, *Studies in the Gospel of Mark*, SCM, London, 1985.

M. Hooker, *St Mark*, Blackwell, London, 1991.

J. Fitzmyer, *Luke the Theologian*, Geoffrey Chapman, London, 1989.

J. Fitzmyer, *St Luke*, Doubleday, New York, 1981–5.

I.H. Marshall, *The Gospel of Luke*, Paternoster, Oxford, 1978.

P. Esler, *Community and Gospel in Luke-Acts*, University Press, Cambridge, 1987.

Fourth Gospel

R. Brown, *The Community of the Beloved Disciple*, G. Chapman, New York/London, 1979.

R. Brown, *The Gospel of John*, Doubleday, New York, 1966–70.

J. Ashton, *Studying John*, Clarendon, Oxford, 1994.

M. Hengel, *The Johannine Question*, SCM, London, 1990.

M. Stibbe, *John's Gospel*, Routledge, London, 1994.

Gospel Themes

A. Richardson, *The Miracle Stories of the Gospels*, SCM, London, 1972 (reprint).

J. Jeremias, *Rediscovering the Parables*, SCM, London, 1966.

E. Schüssler-Fiorenza, *In Memory of Her*, SCM, London, 1983.

M. Barker, *The Gate of Heaven*, SPCK, London, 1991.

The Jesus Literature

H. Köester, *Ancient Christian Gospels*, SCM, London, 1990.

J.H. Hayes and C.R. Holladay, *Biblical Exegesis: A Beginner's Handbook*, SCM, London, 1988.

Selected Further Reading

B. Layton, *The Gnostic Scriptures*, SCM, London, 1987.

J.G. Dunn, *Unity and Diversity in the New Testament*, SCM, London, 1990.

D. McCracken, *The Scandal of the Gospels*, University Press, Oxford, 1994.

Index